Contributors

JANE DILLON spent two years (1969–71) in Milan working for Olivetti, in the studio headed by Ettore Sottsass. Returning to London she set up her own studio (with Charles Dillon, d.1982), and has since combined design work with teaching at the Royal College of Art.

RODNEY GORDON studied at the Hammersmith School of Building and the Architectural Association before joining the LCC in 1957, where he designed the Faraday Memorial at Elephant and Castle. He joined Owen Luder in partnership in 1960, for whom he designed many offices and shopping centres. He designed 66 St James's Street, London, completed in 1979 (with Ray Baum) and is a partner of Tripos Architects.

JONATHON GREEN co-founded *Friends* magazine in the 1960s, and later worked on *OZ*. He recalled the era in a series of interviews first published in 1988, *Days in the Life: Voices from the London Underground 1961–71; All Dressed Up* followed in 1998. He is well known for his writing on slang, including *Slang Down the Ages* (1993), Cassell's *Dictionary of Slang* (1998) and a history of lexicography, *Chasing the Sun* (1996).

ELAIN HARWOOD grew up in Beeston, Notts, where the 1960s meant Radburn housing and new shopping centres rather than chic boutiques. Her introduction to modern architecture was seeing the Nottingham Playhouse pantomime in 1966. She is now the historian at English Heritage responsible for its post-1945 research and listing programme.

PATRICK HODGKINSON is Emeritus Professor of Architecture and Urbanism at the University of Bath. He worked for Alvar Aalto and Felix Samuely before becoming Leslie Martin's chief assistant in 1959, with whom he collaborated on a scheme in West Kentish Town and the first Brunswick Centre project. Since setting up in private practice in 1962 Hodgkinson's other works have included Arts Faculty buildings at Oxford.

JONATHAN HUGHES lectures and publishes on post-war British art and architecture. He recently co-edited the collection of essays *Non-Plan* with Simon Sadler, and is currently researching a monograph on the work of constructionist artist Anthony Hill.

LESLEY JACKSON is a freelance writer, curator and design historian specialising in 20th century design. Her books include *The New Look – Design in the Fifties* (1991);

'Contemporary': *Architecture and Interiors of the 1950s* (1994); *The Sixties – Decade of Design Revolution* (1998); *and Robin and Lucienne Day – Pioneers of Contemporary Design* (2001).

JULES LUBBOCK is Professor of Art History at the University of Essex. His most recent book was *The Tyranny of Taste*, 1995, and he is currently completing a book on early Renaissance narrative painting and sculpture. In 2001 he was awarded a major four-year grant by the Arts and Humanities Research Board to investigate the influence of concepts of personal identity upon post-war architecture and town planning.

KATE MCINTYRE researched the consumption of fashion in the 1960s for her MA dissertation at the Royal College of Art. She writes on many aspects of material culture and is Senior Lecturer in the Faculty of Design, Buckinghamshire Chilterns University College.

SIMON SADLER was born too late in the Sixties to remember it, but one of his earliest architectural memories was of a Sixties' building, when the Liverpool Beacon restaurant gave him his first experience of vertigo. He is now an architectural historian and author of the forthcoming book, *Amazing Archigram*.

PETER SMITHSON, with his wife Alison (1928–93), shaped many of the ideas current in 1960s architecture. The decade saw the realisation of such important buildings as their Economist complex (1964); the Garden Building at St Hilda's College, Oxford (1969); and Robin Hood Gardens, begun in 1968. It also saw the publication of their first books. Most recently, their designs have been collected *in The Charged Void: Architecture* (2002).

GAVIN STAMP can remember the Sixties and he WAS there. He bought his copy of Nairn's *London* at the Elephant and Castle in 1966 – the year he joined the Victorian Society at the age of 18. Since then he has become an architectural historian and Chairman of the Twentieth Century Society, and has written about Lutyens and Giles Scott and even about Ernö Goldfinger and Gillespie, Kidd & Coia, but perhaps his heart really still remains in the 19th century.

SIMON WARTNABY was a 1960s teenage fan of The Beatles, Victorian architecture, the Hayward, Pop Art, *Blow-Up*, and Indica; he now works for English Heritage.

Twentieth Century
Architecture 6

The Sixties

life : style : architecture

EDITED BY ELAIN HARWOOD
AND ALAN POWERS

The Twentieth Century Society
2002

TWENTIETH CENTURY ARCHITECTURE
is published by the Twentieth Century Society
70 Cowcross Street, London EC1M 6EJ
© The authors 2002
The views are those of the authors and not necessarily
of the Society.

NUMBER 6 | 2002 | ISBN O 9529755 6 4 | ISSN 1353–1964

Twentieth Century Architecture Editorial Committee:
Elain Harwood, Alan Powers, Gavin Stamp and
Simon Wartnaby.

Designed and typeset in Utopia
and Egyptian Extended No.4 by Dalrymple
Printed by BAS Printers Ltd.

This Journal was made possible by generous grants from
the Arts Council for England, and from the Paul Mellon
Centre for the Study of British Art.

The Society also gratefully acknowledges a grant from
English Heritage for part of the costs of its casework.

The Twentieth Century Society was founded in 1979 to
promote and preserve architecture and design. To join call
020 7250 3857 or contact www.c20society.org.uk

Contents

Donors

The following contributed most generously to the appeal made following *Twentieth Century Architecture 5: Festival of Britain*, and it is a pleasure to acknowledge so many friends and supporters:

Carolyn Adams, John A. Akroyd, John Alexander, John Allan, W.J.C. Allen, James L. Anderson, Mr & Mrs P.J. Anderson, Mr & Mrs D.M. Archer, Art Deco Society of New South Wales, Norman Ashton, Jane Attias, Mr & Mrs R.C. Bailey, Malcolm R. Bailey, Brian Baker, James & Jackie Ball, Marion & Alan Ball, Tom Ball, Mr & Mrs R.J. Balsdon, Belinda Bamber, John Bancroft, Mrs C. Barclay, Peter Bareham, J. Barker & Dr C. Hubbard, John Alfred Barker, J.G. & K.C. Barnard, Paul Barnfather, Christopher Barry, Marion Barter, Peter Bartle, Alan Baxter, J.F. Bedford, M.C. Bell, P. Bellay, C.R. Bennett, Angela Bennett & Ian Runeckles, L.J. Benstead, John Bentley, Mr & Mrs A.L. Berger, Dr Neil Bingham, Gary Birch, John Black, Sophie Blain, Sylvia Blanc, Revd Norman Boakes, Caroline & Hugh Boileau, Mary Ann Bolger, J.P. Bolter, Derek Bottomley, Gordon and Ursula Bowyer, Richard Bradley, Ian Bradley, Dr Geoff Brandwood, Clive Branson, Blee Ettwein Bridges, Nigel Britton, Louise Brodie, Patrick Brown, Terry Brown, Mr & Mrs Jake Brown, Jane Brown, P.J. Bryan, Felicity Bull, Michael Bullen, Nicholas J. Bush, Lorna Bushell, D.H. Butler, Nicholas Callow, Dr Philip Carter, Elizabeth Casbon, John E. Casey, Peter Cave, Mr & Mrs Geoff Chadwick, Darrell Chalkley, Tim Challans, Alan Chandler, A. Charlton, M.A. Clarke, Bridget Clarke, Roger L. Cline, Robert Close, R.G. Cobb, Tom H.V. Cochrane, Frank Collieson, Neville Conder, Richard Constable, Dr Hazel Conway, Dr Catherine Cooke, Christine & Tim Cookson, Mr & Mrs Denvil Coombe, Mr & Mrs Roger Cooper, A.P. Coopey & T.B. Rawlins, Michael Copeman, Steven Costello, Julia Courtney, Mr & Mrs P.D. Crampton, Diana Crighton, Stephen Croad, John Crowther, Mr & Mrs J.D.H. Cullingham, Mr & Mrs R.L. Cunningham, Dr Elizabeth Darling, Joan Darwent, D.C. Dashwood, David Davidson, Andrew Davies, Nick Dawe & Caroline Gregg, Paul R. Dawson, Peter de Figueiredo, Ray Deahl, Eleanor M. Denton, George H. Derbyshire, C.L. Don, Mr & Mrs M.J. Donegan, Janet Douglas, Robert Drake & Mark Aldbrook, Mrs J. Duddy, Geoffrey & Susan Dudman, Dr J. Duffen, Ian Dungavell, Andy Dunican, James Dunnett, Richard Eckersley, A.F. Eggleston, Peter Elsdon, Mrs A. Holden, Penny Evans, Paul Evans, Mr C. Evans, John Falding, Sir Terry Farrell, Mr & Mrs R.D.L. Felton, Angela S. Filmer, Johnathan Finn, Graham Fisher, Adrian

Forty, Tim Foster, J.E. Francis, Darron Freegard, Jenny Freeman, Philip Froud, Conrad Fry, David Gadsby, Margaret Garlake, Mr & Mrs S. Gath, Kenneth Gay, M. Gaze, Stephen Gee, Lady Gibberd, A.P. Gifford, Maggie Giraud, Alan Girling, Joyce Glasser, Mr & Mrs J. Glennie, Chris Godbold & Trevor Haynes, David Godden & Louise Spalding, Dr & Ms J. Godfrey, B. Godward, Susan Gold, Sheila Goldberg, Edith Gollnast, John Goodricke, Peter Gotlop, Steve Gould, Michael Green, Richard Griffiths, Anthony Grimshaw, Peter Guillery, Barry Guise, Edward Hagger, C.F. Haine & M. Fox, Doreen Halewood, Chris Hall & Louise Hayward, K. & V. Hall, Christopher Hammond, Chris & Carole Hancock, Michael J. Handscomb, K.D. Hanman, Charmain Harbour & Christopher Hawkins, Matthew Hardy, Mrs D. Hargreave, Tom & Felicity Harper, Frank Harris, C.D. Harris, Mr Guy Harrison, Elain Harwood, Harry C. Hatrick, Jonathan N. Hawes, P.G. Hawes, Alan Hayes & Jane Head, David Heath, Mr & Mrs Nicholas Heath, Charlotte Helliwell, Mary Hempstead, A.T. Herbert, Cassie Herschel-Shorland, Helen Hewlett, Deirde Hicks, Alan Higgs, Rosemary Hill, Michael Hill, Peter N. Hirschmann, Miss C.M. Hobbs, Annie Hollobone, Lady Patti Hopkins, Alastair Howe, Peter Howell, Neil Humphrey, Tony Hunt, John & Heather Hunter, John Huntingford, Philip Hurling, Andrew Huxtable, Airlie A. Inglis, John Irving, Lesley Jackson & Ian Fishwick, Sarah Jackson, Neil Jackson, O.G. & J.J. Janssen, David Jarman & Sarah Vickerstaff, Roland J. Jeffery, David Johnson, R. Johnstone, Audrey Jones, Katherine G. Jones, Mr S.R. & Mrs H.M. Jones, Jan Kaplicky, Miss J. Kattenhorn, Anita Keen & Tom Matthews, Frank Kelsall, Jill Kerry, David Kewn, John P. King, Jonathan King, Nicholas W. Kingsley, Epameinondas Kitsos, R. Knight, Iain Langlands, Helen Langley, Daphne Ann Leach, John Leonard, Jill Lever, Edward Lewis, Sarah Lewis, Julian W.S. Litten, David Wharton Lloyd, George E. Loudon, Peter Luckens, Jack Lumley, Jill Lycett, Raymond Magnani, Leonard Manasseh, Kate Mann, S.N.P. Marks, Hugh Martin, Terence Masters, Rick Mather, Alex McColl & Charles Wynn-Evans, Vincent McFarlane, Mrs J. McGregor Smith, A. McIntyre, Ann & Steve McKeown, Alison McKittrick, K.I. McLean, Michael A. Mee, Michael Mellish, Kenneth Mellon, D.G. Middleton, David Mingay & Caron Rohsler, Mrs J. Moller, Jeffrey Montague, C.A. Montellier & W. Bewick, F. Alan Moody, Antonia Moon, J.M. Elaine Mordaunt, Richard & Patricia Mordey, R.J. Morgan, D.J. Morgan, Helen Morley & Stephen Till, Simon Morris, J.L. Morrish,

Dr Timothy Mowl, David Munden, Maggie Murray-Smith, Richard Myall, Dr Gillian Naylor, Steve Oddy & Paul Chamberlain, Sheila Ogilvie, Mrs Y. O'Neill, Dr Seán O'Reilly and Dr Debbie Mays, David Ottewill, Elizabeth Owen, Linda Parry, Tony Partington, I. Patton, Alexander Payne, Eric G. Pearce, P.J. Pearce, Eddy Pearce, Lynn F. Pearson & Sue Hudson, Pauline Pearson, Mr & Mrs R.M. Peel, Mr & Mrs M. Peters, Monica Pidgeon, Mrs E. Pirie, Dr J.R. Pollock, Kenneth Poole, Sir Philip Powell, Peter W.G. Powell, J. Power, Mark Price, M.C. Purdue, Mrs Morfydd Ransom-Hall, Sandy Rattray, Caroline Reed, Anne Reid, Janet Richard, Mark Richards, Margaret and Anthony Richardson, John Richardson, John & Pamela Richardson, Lucienne Roberts & Damian Wayling, J. Max Roberts, Herbert Robinson, Norman Routledge, Mr & Mrs Q. Rubens, Barry Russell, Gillian Sage, Andrew Sanders, Lady Sandilands, Nick Savage, David & Jane Sawyer, Michael Schofield & Anthony Skyrme, Nicholas Serota, Guy Shanley, Ian Shapeero, Molly Shaw, Andrew Shepherd, Jennifer Shields, Derrick Shorten, Stephen Simmons & Suze White, K.A. Slegg & Miss K.M. Egan, Andrew Smith, Brian Smith, David John Smith, Diane Smith, Ian & Eileen Smith, Mr & Mrs S.R. Smith, Mr & Mrs P.J. Snow, Dorothy Sparkes, Maria Speake & Adam Hills, Melvin Spear, Julian Spicer, R. Stallard, Dr Gavin Stamp, A. Starkey, Barrie Stead, Laura Stevens, C. Stocks, Tony Stokoe & Brian Quinn, June A. Stubbs, Helena Sturridge, Roy Sully, C. Swinson, Revd Anthony Symondson sj, Stuart Tappin, Michael Taylor, Dr Roy Taylor, J.A. Terrace, James & Anne Thomas, Nick Thompson, R. Thomson, Philip Thornborow, Robert Thorne, Graham Thorne, Stephen Thorpe, Mrs J. Tilling, P. Todd, Jacqueline Tollit, Mr & Mrs R.C.B. Tomlinson, K.M. Trimmer, P. Tritton, K. Truman, Miss K. Turnbull, Aidan Turner Bishop, Dr Geoffrey Tyack, Peter Urquhart, June Victor, Austin Vince, Christopher Wade, Dr Paul D. Walker, Richard Walker, R.B. Wall, Jonathan Waller, Fiona E. Walmsley-Collins, Dennis Wardleworth, Mrs R.A. Wareham, David and Elaine Warrell, Simon Wartnaby, Fabian Watkinson, Dr & Mr J. Waymark, Mrs K.J. Welham, Dr Volker M. Welter, Vala West, Westminster Libraries, Mrs M. Wiggins, Dr D.G. Wild, J.A. Wilkinson, Peter Willis, Elizabeth Wilson, Muriel Wilson, H.A. Winch, Michael Winchester & Anna Trojanowski, John Winter, Brian and Leta Woodcock, Mr & Mrs Mark Woodford, Elizabeth C. Woods, Dr Giles Worsley, J.R. Wrangham, Sarah Yates, Mrs M.J. Yeats, J.E.M. Yorke, Carola Zogolovitch.

Foreword

ELAIN HARWOOD AND ALAN POWERS

April 1997 was a strange month in Britain. Eighteen years of Conservative government might or might not have been about to come to an end, and against this background of hopeful uncertainty, the Twentieth Century Society held its conference on the Sixties. Perhaps the mood resembled that in early 1964, as thirteen years of Tory rule ended amid accusations of sleaze, to be replaced by the disenchanting pragmatism of Harold Wilson.

The event took its place in a sequence, starting with the two-day conference 'Refashioning the Fifties' in September 1992, and a later conference on the Seventies in April 1999. The Sixties event was spread over a three-day weekend in London, and carried on with a further two days in Birmingham. Jonathon Green's brilliant talk 'All dressed up', delivered on a sunny Saturday morning at the Royal Festival Hall, acknowledged that much that happened in the Sixties was silly, but found that it was after all a 'useable past', and after so long and strenuous a period of rejection, a little innocent idealism might not come amiss. It may have been a daft idea, but we had a Sixties disco on the Friday night at John Bancroft's Pimlico School, a famous building of the decade then under threat of replacement by a PFI development, with Gavin Stamp as the DJ. On the Saturday evening, a select group went to the Roundhouse where there was a giant white 'bouncy castle' for adults. You could not get much more Sixties than that.

There was a festive feeling to this conference, which has provided the majority of the pieces in this publication. Taking the title 'Sixties: life style architecture', the aim was to place architecture in a broader context of visual culture. Some of the speakers, designers such as Jane Dillon, Peter Smithson, Patrick Hodgkinson and Rodney Gordon, were revisiting the period of their early professional life; others, such as Elain Harwood, were bringing the interpretative tools of historians to understand phenomena lived through in childhood. Gavin Stamp split the difference, looking both critically and nostalgically at the links between the neo-Victorian fashions of the period and the more serious business of conservation. Jules Lubbock reappraised his experience of living and teaching at Essex University, thirty years on. In Birmingham, the perils and wonders of car-driven urban regeneration were reviewed, and Jonathan Hughes showed how motor transport was the metaphor not only for cities but for hospitals.

It was not possible to publish everything from so large a conference, and regrettably a number of papers have had to be omitted from this publication. We thank the authors of these just the same for the contribution they made to a memorable event. We would like to thank Paul Atterbury, Geoffrey Broadbent, Nicola Coxon, Catherine Croft, Andrew Higgott, Bob Jarvis, Michael Manser, Cynthia Weaver, and the other contributors whose personal memories and re-appraisals did not adapt to articles. The pieces by Lesley Jackson, who was a speaker at the conference, and Kate McIntyre and Simon Sadler, who were not, have been specially written for this publication. We are also indebted to all those who helped organise and run the conference, and specially Eva Ling, Nicola Coxon, David Davidson, Marina Vaizey, Ken Powell and Laura Iloniemi. Robert Elwall and Jonathan Makepiece at the RIBA Library photograph collection and Judith Caul at *The Guardian* have been very helpful. English Heritage has generously permitted the use of its photographs, and for us to reproduce de Jong's view of Old London Bridge, now at Kenwood. The conference was generously supported by the Arts Council's Architecture Unit, as is the present publication, which has also benefited from a grant from the Paul Mellon Centre for the Study of British Art.

Particular thanks are due to Anthea Streeter, who diligently transcribed the tapes and liaised with the speakers. They have been very patient in waiting until well into a second Labour term to see the publication come to fruition.

We are not so naïve in the 21st century, as even Tony Blair must realise. But the Sixties still hold a sway as no other recent decade, for it was the time when youth found its distinctive voice. That the generation gap may be closing – that the youth of today find it harder to rebel – is due to the lasting impact of Sixties' liberalisation in every aspect of life. But it is still exciting to see just how the legends were made.

1 | All Dressed Up:
The Sixties 'Youth Revolution'
in retrospect

JONATHON GREEN

All Dressed Up: The Sixties 'Youth Revolution' in retrospect

JONATHON GREEN

It was, I believe, in 1971 that *Rolling Stone* magazine, purveyor of rock's holy writ to the eager masses, canvassed the ex-Beatle John Lennon for his opinions on the Sixties, a decade in which he had played so leading a role. Being Lennon and touting his 'rebel' image, his response was suitably mordant: 'What happened in the Sixties,' he declared, 'was that we all dressed up.' It was meant, in Lennon style, as a putdown, a cheap and cheerful dismissal of an era that had made him – and in fairness he'd help make – but despite his professed disdain Lennon's crack had a certain pertinence. Certainly for me. For it is my belief – that Lennon, as such emblematic figures should, got it absolutely right. What happened in the Sixties was just that: we all dressed up.

The phrase, it seems to me, works on a variety of levels. The most obvious is the dressing up of the seemingly endless party that made its merry way through Swinging London, flower power, rock festivals, and the whole gaudy panoply of the popular myth of the period. This England swung, as the American folk singer Roger Miller put it, 'like a pendulum do.' This was the world of Union Jack knickers (possibly edible), of 'I'm Backing Britain', of Prime Minister Wilson handing over MBEs to the Beatles (and their smoking dope in the Buckingham Palace lavatories), in the shortest of shorthand, of Carnaby Street.

For those who position the period as the first step on some downward path, the slippery slope that leads to cultural hell, any thoughts of characterising it as a joyful, celebratory era are anathema. But looking back, you can't dismiss the party element. After the self-denial of the Second World War and the period of austerity that followed, after the struggle towards mass consumerism that typified the Fifties (not quite so grey, perhaps, as they are traditionally painted, but hardly the most blithe of decades) there is an element of dressing up, of party-time about the decade that followed. For some it was 'party best', for others full-scale fancy dress, while for many, noses pressed to the window, it was merely the reflection, alluring or repellent, of those so dead-set on their good time.

But there are other nuances. Forget the 'dressed up', what I believe really matters is the 'all'. If the party image underpins the ephemeral side of the Sixties, the period's social engineering is what has lasted. In this context I would interpret 'dressing up' as meaning the enjoyment of social rights, especially those that reflect on our private lives. Far more important, and longer-lasting than its party image, is the role of the Sixties as a period of unrivalled democratisation. It is arguable that there was much less actually new than might have appeared. Certainly if one had the right connections, the right social standing, and especially the right money, one could always procure a divorce, an abortion, conduct a homosexual affair, or read a forbidden book. In so class-ridden a society as Britain's the rich and powerful had always operated under different constraints to the masses. What happened in the Sixties was that thanks to a range of social legislation – the Obscene Publications Act, divorce and abor-

Figure 1. Carnaby Street decorations, Christmas 1967 (*The Guardian*, photographer Peter Jones)

tion law reform, a compromised but still revolutionary change in attitudes towards homosexuality – such freedoms became far more generally available. Like some paternalistically liberal Fairy Godfather, Roy Jenkins, then Home Secretary and determined advocate of all such measures, informed us that this party, once so exclusive, was one we could all enjoy. As he put it, rebutting the inevitable critics, 'the permissive society is the civilized society.'

And there's a final side of the image. The unspoken words that tend to follow 'all dressed up' are usually 'and nowhere to go'. It's an easy jibe, but it does need addressing. After the ball, after the party, you wake in the grim dawn with a hangover and a bedmate whose name you never did quite catch. What happened to all that celebration?

The answer is that we live in the shadow of the Sixties. Of all the artificial constructs by which we delineate our immediate past, the Sixties have the greatest purchase on the mass imagination. They stand, rightly or not, as the dominant myth of the modern era. That you might have been too old or too young to enjoy them – indeed, that you might not even have been born – is of marginal importance. The great edifice casts its shadow and everything must seek its own light within it.

So what, you might ask, were the Sixties? When did the period start, when did it finish? As far as chronology goes, there's a raft of suggestions. Some claim 1956 as the launching pad, that *annus mirabilis* of Suez, Hungary and John Osborne's *Look Back in Anger*. Others opt for 1957, the publication of the beatnik classic *On the Road* (and Jack Kerouac was writing of events already ten years old), or 1958, the first Aldermaston march and the birth of CND. Then there's 1961, the Committee of 100 and the Spies for Peace; 1963, the Profumo Affair, Beatlemania, the Kennedy assassination, the birth of 'satire' with *Private Eye* and TV's '*That Was the Week That Was*'; 1964, the election of the first Labour government after what the propaganda proclaimed as 'thirteen years of Tory misrule'; even 1965, when every beatnik which the country could muster turned up to listen to Allen Ginsberg at the Albert Hall.

As for the closure of the Sixties, the more diehard beats, deeply unhappy with the new generation of rebels, saw it as that same Albert Hall poetry reading; then there's 1967, the 'Summer of Love' and the first mass-marketing of the alternative society; 1971, the trial of *OZ* magazine; 1974, the oil embargo and latest onset of economic decline; even 1977, the high noon of punk rock and for all its loathing of hippies a Sixties manifestation if ever there was one. The sole truth is that there are no cut and dried lines. The most important role of all those dates is that within them you can discern some of the main impulses and events that drove the period.

In the end the Sixties, to steal a description first allotted to New York's Greenwich Village, are as much a state of mind as a chronological concept. And like all states of mind they are open to myriad interpretations. In the years that have followed the very concept of the period has caused as intense a polarisation in retrospect as ever it did when the contentious events were actually going on. For some they remain 'the best years of our lives'; for others the end of civilisation as we know it. Neither is wholly right, but ignorance has never stood in the way of zealotry. For the nay-sayers, there is little to consider here. You can't dismiss their views – after all it is their belated triumph that has created the country in which we live today – but at the time they represented little more than the impotent bleating of the fearful and the threatened. The point of the Sixties is change – realised or otherwise, feasible or foolhardy. Remember the old slogan: 'Are you part of the problem or part of the solution?' The spokespeople for the problem were as vapidly obvious then as they are vainglorious now.

As for the advocates, over-optimistic and naive they may have been, but they did offer hope. Their theories may have been vague, ill-worked out and positively absurd at times, but they looked forward to a possible future, rather than backwards to a long-dead, equally fantastical past. Above all they were utopians. They believed quite genuinely that the world actually could be made a better place. To quote *Days in the Life*, my own oral history of the period:

> '*Embarrassingly earnest at times, gleefully unimpressed by the trappings of economic stability and the bottom line, the "freaks" set determinedly about their regenerative task much as their mothers might take over the Oxfam bring-and-buy. Crusading zeal to the fore, they plunged in undeterred, taking full advantage of the optimism of the times. Much of it was naive, a good deal simply psychedelic pipe-dreams, but much too was achieved. A more sceptical approach might have avoided the more ludicrous blunders, but a more sceptical approach would have missed out on the undeniable successes.*'

There are various reasons for such optimism, not the least of them youthful enthusiasm. But paradoxically, for so outwardly anti-parental a generation, one reason at least seems to spring from the past. The young of the period had been brought up by parents whose own formative experience had been the Second World War. Unlike many such conflicts, this was categorized as a 'good war'; those who survived it came home as heroes, they had 'saved the world from fascism' and, willy-nilly, 'made it a better place'. Whatever the realities that followed, the Labour landslide in the General Election of 1945 was a triumph of utopian belief. Despite the obligatory antagonism of the 'generation gap' (a concept that was satisfactorily coined in that *echt*-Sixties year, 1967), the young people who made the Sixties were infused with that same optimism. Their parents had done it their way, why should not the children follow suit? The assumption of endlessly unfolding progress is sadly tarnished today; then it was still in place. Prime Minister Harold Macmillan had boasted that 'You've never had it so good.' The young were keen to prove him wrong.

The struggle was different, the 'enemy' was much nearer home, but the bottom line seems strikingly similar: changing things for the better. It can't just be coincidence that the word 'fascist' was disinterred from the textbooks and brandished so enthusiastically by a generation whose parents had supposedly purged it from the modern political vocabulary.

But this is hindsight and if the Sixties generation really did owe a debt to their parents, then it was largely subconscious. Of one thing there is no doubt: the Sixties generation was quite genuinely something new; a post-war phenomenon that had simply not existed prior to 1950 and wouldn't really start making its mark for another ten years. If the phrase 'generation gap' had appeared as recently as 1967, then the word 'teenager' was barely a couple of decades older. 'Adolescence', teen's predecessor, had existed since the early fifteenth century. It meant simply: becoming an adult. It was a passage, not a status. 'Teenage' conferred that status. One lingered; indeed, moving on was a regret and no reward. The years between thirteen and twenty had always existed, but never in so totemic and autonomous a way. Prior to the Fifties they represented little more than a necessary way-station – no longer a child, not yet an adult. Henceforth, in the post-war decades, teenage life began its gradual move to centre-stage.

The teens of the Fifties were essentially aping the parental lifestyle. The most important factor was the gaining of one's own income – one spent it on consumption and on carving out a small corner of the world for oneself – but there was little impetus to change the overall culture, merely to colonise a small section. As the Fifties proceeded, that changed. Working class teens moved through a number of cults, most importantly those of Teddy Boys and later Mods. The more rebellious of their middle-class peers, apostrophised conveniently as Beatniks, began to shift into preoccupations that took them far from the pre-ordained world of the professions or 'a good job'. All moved inexorably beyond the adult world. It is as if there arose a gradual, ever-intensifying sense of one's own potential. And as the state of mind known as 'the Sixties' came up to speed, fuelled by that triumvirate of dope, sex and rock 'n' roll, plus the non-specific but perennially popular concept of 'revolution', there developed what has to be acknowledged as an 'alternative' society.

That society, synonymously self-described as the 'underground' or the 'counter-culture', was not, by the standards of the larger world, either clandestine or revolutionary. It was more, to quote the sociologist Talcott Parsons, an 'expressive revolution': disillusioned with the mainstream, hungry for new experience, encouraged by Herbert Marcuse and Norman O. Brown, by Allen Ginsberg and Bob Dylan, dedicated to 'doing its own thing'. And, compared with the synthetic, commercialised labels of 'Swinging London' or 'The Beautiful People', it mattered. In an era of instant myth, the 'underground' could claim genuine cohesion and as much if not greater validity than that gaudy offspring of a *Time* magazine writer's fantasies or a caravan-borne procession of paisley-clad aristos.

It was an educated movement, drawing primarily on the alienated children of the comfortable bourgeoisie, from which background it drew its strength – the middle-class confidence that the world existed for its convenience and should be treated as such – and its weakness, the inevitable elitism that put off many 'ordinary' youngsters. The counter-culture chose to stand against the consumerism of the era, offering a parallel and quite contrary nirvana to what Prime Minister Wilson called the 'white heat' of the technological revolution. It was not overtly political, preferring to mock both the old and new left, but it adopted a predictably liberal platform, backing abortion law reform, the abolition of censorship, sexual freedom of no matter what persuasion, banning the bomb and of course the legalisation of soft drugs. Imbued with Modernism, many of its preoccupations, albeit in their elite, far from democratized form, can be found in the precious salons of what had been known as 'Bloomsbury'. They too had opted for soft-left politics, for free love, the occasional drug, the 'getting it together' in their country cottages, and above all the ultimate importance of personal emotion.

The Sixties had its own media – newspapers, magazines, film, theatre, and video. A large section of the rock industry was targeted straight at it. It had advice centres and self-help groups of every hue. For those who fancied an alternative brand of 'venture capitalism' there was the world of drug selling, and for those more respectful of the law a whole range of craft and cottage industries. It had restaurants, food shops, clubs and outfitters. And at its tribal gatherings, the great rock festivals, tens of thousands claimed allegiance to its ranks.

None of which was exactly 'teenage'. The hippie hardcore were in their early twenties, there was a substantial infusion of Americans and Australians who were older still, not to mention such grown-up fellow-travellers as the critic Ken Tynan or the 'anti-psychiatrist' R.D. Laing. The feel was student rather than schoolchild, but the prevailing ethos was undeniably geared towards the desire to oust the adult world. But even the mainstream developments – a Labour government, liberal social legislation, a change in music, in fashion, in architecture, in the food we cooked and ate, the holidays we took and so much more – were all rooted, perhaps less noisily, in the desire for what I'd call 'cultural patricide'.

Of its various stimuli an important one was simply novelty. After all, the mere concept of such an 'alternative' (at least on so large a scale) had only just come into existence and the very fact of putting such a concept into effect was exciting enough. Today's young may appear to have abandoned such efforts, but their task is so much harder. Three decades back it was very simple to shock. The idea that 'no-one had done it before' is central to the impact of the

Sixties. This was something of an illusion because every generation thinks it has invented the world, but it was one that society was willing to accept. Taken one by one, most of the cultural 'revolutions' were not in themselves new: one had been able to procure an abortion, to utilise contraception, to take recreational drugs, to read illicit literature, to divorce and to indulge in same-sex relationships. But one had not been able to do any of it very openly, and in most cases one had not been able to do it very easily without money. (Contraception was different: the exclusivity there came from gender rather than income.) The complaisant doctor, whether wielding syringe or curette; the locked cabinet of 'curiosae'; the discreet cohabitation of a pair of 'confirmed bachelors' – such things were the perks of the middle classes and above. Of course there had been vegetarians, feminists, commune-dwellers, free-lovers, British Buddhists and plenty more before, but these were easily dismissed as 'cranks'.

What the Sixties tore down was a world of real Victorian values: a world of deference, of knowing one's place. It had lasted well into the Fifties and in some ways remains. What the Sixties *brought* was a democratisation of such things – the end to a value system that, for all the buffetings it had endured, had stood in place for more than a century. It was that, as much as any intrinsic moral yeas or nays, that created so much of the hostility. In many ways the critics were right to worry; it was indeed the end of their ordered, hierarchical, deferential world.

Such democracy, of course, was instantly associated with America, and the concept and lifestyle that would become known as 'teenage' were far from all that made the transatlantic trip. Among the many currents running through the Sixties is that America and its ways were 'where it was at'. That went for the government, desperate to maintain the 'special relationship', as much as it did for the counter-culture. The nineteenth century may have offered Britain its imperial moment, but its successor went cap in hand across the Atlantic. Mass culture, popular culture, however one termed it, this was America's unrivalled gift. It wasn't always especially welcome: few celebrate their own death warrant, and Britain has yet to come happily to terms with America's cultural power. But America was what mattered and even the downside was important: the very absence of America's war in Vietnam ensured that England's 'counter-culture', try as it might, would always be less vibrant. Still, a good deal of homegrown input remained. 'Swinging London' may have been conjured up by a bunch of *Time* magazine editors, apparently searching for a way of getting more mini-skirted dollybirds into the magazine, but it was London they feted, not New York. Then as now Britain offered a level of pure style that dazzled Americans. In addition there was British rock 'n' roll, the 'English invasion', as the media put it. Even the average US teen was perfectly happy with Herman's Hermits singing *I'm 'Enery the eighth I am*. Yet even here America had the last word. Everybody bought the elite – The Beatles, The Stones, The Who, Cream and all the rest – but in the end what were the white British boys doing other than recycling the music of the black American men and making it palatable for the mass market?

For the 'underground' proper, the culture was a one-way street, and it began in the States. Only the lefties looked to Europe. As far as America went, they might have puffed, but they rarely dared inhale. Perhaps they were right: there was something 'ersatz' about Britain's espousal of the US scene. For instance you could read *On the Road* but Land's End to John O'Groats was hardly New York to San Francisco. But you could dream, and many did. In the end you either had Vietnam or you didn't. And without it even the most angry of protests couldn't fill their hollow centre.

All parties must end. The end of the Sixties party was well overdue and no matter what end-date you may choose, on 3 May 1979 it really was time to call it a day. Nanny, that loved and loathed figment of the national psyche, may have been on holiday, but now she was back, with a vengeance. The last die-hard, desperate celebrants, puffing on their roaches, downing the very dregs of long-emptied bottles, were finally turfed out into the unwelcoming dawn of a very different day. It had been enormous fun, a glorious melee into which had been poured all the energies, all the creativity, all the hopes of a generation who foolishly but quite genuinely believed that they could change the world. If they failed, it was not through lack of trying. And in some areas they did succeed, not perhaps as they might have envisaged, but theirs was not just empty noise.

At the start of a new century it is hard not to see the Sixties, at least in cultural terms, as a pivotal decade. It was not the most momentous – although I would suggest that in purely social terms none surpassed it – and its perceived importance can be put down to the current access to the media of those whose youth was played out against its gaudy wallpaper. But for all the sounds and furies of the Twenties and the Thirties, the years of the two World Wars, the grim, destructive Eighties (self-interested philistinism masquerading as national regeneration), and the beleaguered, directionless, millennial Nineties, the Sixties seem to stand in the centre of it all, sucking in the influences of the past, creating the touchstones of the future. Certainly what has appeared since is consistently measured against the era – whether in the nostalgia it evokes, or in its demonisation. So much of the last two decades was the revenge of the have-nots, the triumph of the grey: those who were either left uninvited to the party, or felt themselves unequal to its delights, and now finally, if perhaps temporarily, ascendent.

Perhaps, as Richard Neville, the editor of *OZ* magazine, was at pains to explain, the 'alternatives' were never that important. They were merely one more example of the pleasure principle, and at best the counter-culture was only 'playing at work', but that didn't diminish its substance. At its height the underground was unavoidably there, promoting and living out its parallel universe. And if today it appears as some madly skittering comet, flashing speedily across the cultural sky, its legacy cannot be denied. The changes that took place in British society in the Sixties did not all spring from the underground but many of them can be traced directly to hippie inspiration. At the time they seemed highly revolutionary, at least that's what Establishment reaction implied. Today they've been absorbed into mainstream British life: fringe theatres, art centres, natural food stores, a host of cottage industries and workers' co-operatives; a concern for the environment and its ecology; the personal politics of gay liberation and the women's movement; the squatting movement and its legacy of housing action groups; the obsession with a clean, healthy body, and the variety of alternative physical and mental therapies. Even the do-nothing hedonism has been perpetuated in the 'Slackers' of recent years. And as for drugs … They all may be under siege, but they're there. Pandora's Box, it should be recalled, contained not evil, but wisdom; try as the revisionists and demonisers may, they will not shut it again.

'The only thing that happened in the Sixties was that we all dressed up'. However he may have meant it, we need not see John Lennon's comment as simply dismissive. It serves as a better postscript than many lines that have followed. And as for now, as an unregenerate fan of that long-gone era, I can but paraphrase the Romantic poet Shelley, that ur-Sixties man with his free love, his opium, his ambiguous feminism and his unresolved revolution. 'Look on her works ye mighty, and despair'. He meant Ozymandias, that mighty, fallen monarch, but he could have been looking at modern Britain.

2 | Fab Fash Pop – 'the look' of British Design during the early 1960s

LESLEY JACKSON

Fab Fash Pop – 'the look' of British Design during the early 1960s

LESLEY JACKSON

In April 1964 *The Ambassador* (the trade magazine of the British textile industry) ran a feature called 'Fab Fash Pop' on a group of up-and-coming young British fashion designers. Mini dresses and catsuits by Mary Quant, Foale & Tuffin, Jean Muir and Emmanuelle Khan were modelled against the backdrop of an exhibition by the American artist Robert Rauschenberg at the Whitechapel Art Gallery. The article celebrated the revolution in British fashion, and the triumph of youth-orientated 'ready-to-wear' on the international market. 'Fab Fash Pop' suggested that this new-found confidence in British fashion was closely allied to the success of British Pop.

During the early 1960s British design, like British fashion and music, was infused with a new spirit of energy and enthusiasm, manifested in a wave of dynamic creativity and the emergence of a distinctive Pop and fashion-linked aesthetic. Furniture, furnishings and domestic products all flowered during this period. The booming economy and the upbeat mood of the nation's youth, symbolised by Carnaby Street, fed directly into the design of everyday goods. The designers who led this push had mostly trained during the early to mid 1950s – many at the Royal College of Art – and were still at an early stage in their careers. Full of enthusiasm, they embraced the commercial and creative opportunities that were opening up as Britain's economy bounced back after the war.

Just as, in describing developments during the late 1940s and early 1950s, a phrase derived from French haute couture – 'The New Look' introduced by Christian Dior – sums up the character of the new post-war style, so during the early 1960s, a phrase originating from British fashion – 'the look' pioneered by Mary Quant – defines the revolution in outlook and aesthetics. The choice of lower case typography is significant, denoting informality and a break with tradition. It confirms the crucial shift away from high style – by implication expensive and adult – to more casual, youthful, affordable and democratic styles of design directed at the mass market.

The 1960s was a much more complex decade in design terms than the 1950s, with several apparently conflicting things happening concurrently or in rapid succession. After the Second World War architects and designers from as far afield as Italy, Scandinavia, the United States and Britain seemed to converge in their creative thinking, and the relaxed but visually stimulating 'Contemporary' style came spontaneously into being. From the late 1940s onwards, and throughout the ensuing decade, 'Contemporary' – a self-consciously modern aesthetic which combined elements of Modernism with expressive form and decoration – became the shared international language of architects and designers, acting as a unifying force at such diverse events as the Festival of Britain, the Milan Triennales and the Brussels Expo.

But if the 1950s are remarkable for their coherence and convergence, the opposite is true of the 1960s, the latter part of which was characterised by divergence and fragmentation. Just as, during the 1950s, the design climate was strongly influenced by circumstances in the wider world – the sudden out-

Figure 1. *Studio* coffee pot designed by Tom Arnold for J. & G. Meakin, featuring *Aztec* pattern, 1964

pouring of pent-up creativity after almost a decade of frustration and restraint during the war – so developments in design during the late 1960s parallel the widespread civil unrest of the period – the protests of the world's youth against the oppressive forces of the establishment. However, this article focuses on the calm before the storm, the surge of creativity in Britain during the early years of the decade before dissolution and disillusion set in. This period was just as revolutionary as the late 1960s, but at this stage radicalism was expressed in positive, creative terms, rather than through dissent.

On an international level the supreme design superpower of the 1960s was Italy. It was in Italy that the full potential of plastics – the ultimate Space Age material – was exploited most comprehensively. Drawing on a range of hard and soft plastics, the Italians realised in sculptural form what designers in most other countries could only dream of. It was in Italy, too, that many of the most potent new technological and ideological concepts about design were formulated, embodied in the remarkable furniture of Joe Colombo, the multifarious proto-Post-Modernist activities of Ettore Sottsass, and the radical insurgence of avant-garde groups such as Superstudio and Archizoom. What the Italians formulated during the 1960s was not just an updated version of 'Contemporary', but a 'New Domestic Landscape'; hence the title of a landmark exhibition held at the Museum of Modern Art in New York in 1972, marking the culmination of a decade of creative ferment.

However, the Italian design explosion of the 1960s is not the subject of this article, which focuses instead on the crystallisation of a new design aesthetic in Britain, and the characteristics of that style. According to my calculations, 'the look' arrived in Britain around 1962, neatly coinciding with The Beatles. This was the year that Robin Day began developing his ground-breaking polypropylene chair for Hille, a robust, utilitarian, low-cost, multi-functional people's chair, the first in the world to use injection-moulded polypropylene for the shell of a seat. Polypropylene, which is light, supple and extremely durable, marked a significant advance on fibreglass (or more correctly, thermosetting resin reinforced with fibreglass), the rather brittle and heavy material used by Charles Eames for his pioneering moulded shell chair the previous decade. By harnessing the hitherto untapped potential of polypropylene, Robin Day liberated low-cost furniture production, and his achievements won him international acclaim and recognition.

Trained at the RCA during the mid 1930s, Robin Day's career as a furniture designer had had to be put on hold during the war. In 1948, however, he and Clive Latimer won the International Low-Cost Furniture Competition organised by the Museum of Modern Art for an innovative range of moulded plywood storage cabinets. Day was subsequently awarded a high profile contract to design the seating for the Royal Festival Hall, and his career in Britain flourished from this date onwards after he teamed up with the supportive firm, Hille. Moulded plywood shells supported by steel rod legs formed the basis of his early chair designs, which were gently sculptural and organic in aesthetic. Because these materials were so strong, it meant that they could be used in thin layers and narrow gauges, giving a light, sprightly appearance to Day's designs. Although he absorbed stylistic influences from the United States and Denmark, Day was never one for unnecessary visual flourishes, and it was his disciplined, economical approach that distinguished his designs.

One of the advantages of using polypropylene in place of moulded plywood was that it allowed for much greater subtlety in shaping the profile of the seat. Technologically Day's design marked a huge step forward, because the moulded plastic seat was strong enough not to require additional reinforcements, and the metal legs could be screwed directly into the underside of the shell. Launched in 1964, the polypropylene chair has remained in continuous production right up to the present day. Within a short space of time, it began spawning look-alikes – always a sure sign of a successful design – notably in a copycat version produced by PEL. Advertisements for the polypropylene chair, and the innumerable later variants that Day subsequently developed for Hille, continued to appear in architecture and design magazines for the remainder of the decade, and it was often cited as an example of Pop design. The adoption of plastics paved the way for bold experimentation with colour, and the polypropylene chair was originally produced in three colours, including an orange-red called flame. Unlike some of the more ambitious but ephemeral furniture experiments of the period, the polypropylene chair has lasted, both physically and stylistically. In fact it has proved to be virtually indestructible, a rare claim for any piece of furniture, especially one from the post-war period.

Although it is for his plastic chairs that Robin Day is best known, he continued to design in wood throughout the 1960s, a material to which he remained lastingly committed. His teak dining chairs and tables for the newly built Churchill College, Cambridge (1964), provide a good example of the robust, rectilinear structures and rich dark colours that he favoured in this medium, an aesthetic evolved to complement the forms and textures of contemporary architecture. Robin Day's dual interest in brightly coloured, sculptural, plastic forms, and chunky, block-like, wooden shapes, reflects the dichotomy in 'the look' of British furniture during early 1960s. Space Age shapes and materials were only one side of the coin.

One place where these two complementary aesthetics were actively promoted side by side was Habitat, the youth-orientated furniture and furnishings store established by Terence Conran in 1964. It was Conran's experience as a textile and furniture designer and manufacturer during the 1950s that eventually prompted him to establish his own retail outlet, which rapidly took off and grew into a chain. He sensed the growing interest amongst the young in all aspects of modern design, not just fashion. Habitat ensured that his

Figure 2. Advertisement for high chair and bar stool versions of the polypropylene chair designed by Robin Day for Hille, May 1967

Figure 3. Advertisement for furniture produced by Conran + Company, May 1964

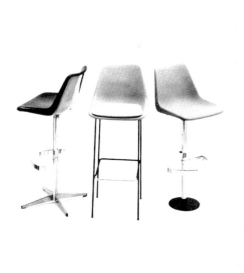

Pop up upon a Polyprop...

hille

pythagoras is more than just a theorem

Conran + Company Limited

Figure 4. Advertisement for *Fine* tableware designed by Roy Midwinter and David Queensberry for Midwinter, 1961, featuring *Queensberry Stripe* pattern designed by David Queensberry, 1962

products – and others in a similar vein – reached their target market. It was all part of the process of the democratisation of design.

If the polypropylene chair was embraced as the people's chair and Habitat was adopted as the people's shop, then the people's pots were the tall cylindrical tablewares of Midwinter, Meakin, Portmeirion and Denby. Midwinter's *Fine* range, co-designed by Roy Midwinter and David Queensberry, became an instant success as soon as it appeared on the market in 1962. With its can-shaped vessel forms and crisply detailed patterns, *Fine* marked a significant departure from the sweeping curvilinear shapes and fluid patterns of Midwinter's *Fashion* range of 1955. Although produced in low-cost, low-fired earthenware, the body of *Fine* was so white and thin that it resembled expensive, high-fired porcelain. The range was also distinguished by the use of overglaze-enamel printed patterns, instead of hand-painted underglaze decoration, which gave the pots a more sophisticated and polished appearance.

Susan Williams-Ellis's teeteringly tall, narrow, cylindrical *Totem* coffee pot (1962) for Portmeirion Pottery with its spindly handles and spouts, and Gill Pemberton's robust stoneware *Chevron* tableware (1963) for Denby, were also a resounding success during the early 1960s. Although different in colour, texture and weight, both were decorated with precise geometric motifs, and combined relief-textured patterns with monochrome glazes. Attenuated tube-shaped vessels such as these – the ceramic equivalent of Twiggy in a Mary Quant shift dress – typified 'the look' of 1960s tableware. As it turned out, such tall pots proved rather impractical to use. But J. & G. Meakin came up with the ideal solution, their elegant but practical *Studio* range (c.1964) designed by Tom Arnold. Its shape was a toned down version of Portmeirion's *Totem*, and its patterns similar in style to those on Midwinter's *Fine*.

David Queensberry, who played a key role in developing 'the look' of 1960s tableware, had been appointed Professor of Ceramics and Glass at the RCA in 1959. In addition to Midwinter, he also helped to update the image of several other firms during the 1960s. His strikingly modern range of cut glass vases and bowls for Webb Corbett, in which straight-sided cylindrical vessel shapes were decorated with diamond, grid and circle patterns, was a worthy recipient of the Design Council's Duke of Edinburgh Award for Elegant Design in 1964.

Fashion was moving at such a rapid rate during the 1960s that manufacturers had to keep on their toes to stay on top of the market. Whitefriars Glass, a perennially forward-looking company, updated its products on a regular basis throughout the decade to reflect the evolution of 'the look'. During the 1950s Whitefriars had followed the Scandinavian model, producing thick-walled, freeform vessels that exploited the plasticity of molten glass. In 1962, however, Geoffrey Baxter, the younger of Whitefriars' two designers, initiated a change of tack. Co-opting turn mould-blowing techniques previously reserved for producing lampshades, Baxter designed a range of thin-walled vases produced in dark inky colours such as midnight blue and shadow green. These pieces, with their clean-lined angular shapes, were succeeded in turn by the so-called *Knobbly Range* (1964) designed by William Wilson, which combined streaky colours with irregular forms and lumpy surface effects. The runaway success of the decade, however, was Geoffrey Baxter's *Textured Range* (1967), a collection of deliberately ungainly mould-blown vessels with coarse bark and wood patterned surfaces. Produced initially in subtle cinnamon, willow and indigo, they looked even more remarkable in their later psychedelic guise of tangerine and kingfisher blue.

Another area of British design in which textured effects were explored during the 1960s, along with cylindrical and angular shapes, was metalwork, which underwent a transformation comparable to that of ceramics and glass. The decade was dominated by a trio of talented silversmiths – Robert Welch, Gerald Benney and David Mellor – who had all trained together at the RCA

spell of Jackson Pollock, was also on its way out by 1962. The mood, although still energetic and upbeat, suddenly turned serious, as designers vied to create gigantic, hard-edged, geometric patterns for the large picture windows of schools and foyers. Countering all this earnestness was the lure of Carnaby Street, which triggered off an avalanche of dazzling Op patterns and riotous flat floral designs.

Along with Heal Fabrics, another major player in the field of printed furnishing fabrics during the 1960s was the smaller firm of Hull Traders. Established in 1957, Hull Traders was strongly allied with the contemporary art world, initially through its relationship with Eduardo Paolozzi and Nigel Henderson. The appointment of Shirley Craven as chief designer and art director in 1960 heralded a decade of outstanding innovation. Over the next ten years the company produced a series of uncompromisingly original designs. Craven's *Division*, which combined geometric abstraction with painterly freedom, won a Design Centre Award in 1964. Her designs were distinguished not only by their imaginative compositions, but their unusual colour combinations.

British wallpaper design was also on a high at the start of the 1960s. The renowned Palladio range, first introduced by the Wall Paper Manufacturers (WPM) in 1955, continued to evolve in interesting ways throughout the 1960s, in spite of the enforced break-up of the WPM by the Monopolies Commission. Designed specifically for architects, the Palladio collections showcased ambitious, large-scale patterns in a range of modern styles. In 1960 the Palladio range was still being produced by the Lightbown Aspinall branch of the WPM, with art direction by Roger Nicholson. Production was later transferred to Sanderson, and artistic control passed to the WPM's newly established Central Design Studio, initially run by Deryck Healey, subsequently by Edward Pond. This accounts for the stylistic evolution of the Palladio collections over the course of the decade. They started out as a vehicle for designers of painterly and architectural persuasions, but later reflected diverse fashions, including Op, Pop and Flower Power.

Throughout the 1960s there were interesting parallels between the career of The Beatles and the development of British design. The Beatles were a product

Figure 8. *Piazza* screen-printed cotton furnishing fabric designed by Barbara Brown for Heal Fabrics, 1964

Figure 9. *Cadenza* screen-printed cotton furnishing fabric designed by Lucienne Day for Heal Fabrics, 1962

Figure 10. Advertisement for *Impact* screen-printed cotton furnishing fabric designed by Evelyn Brooks for Heal Fabrics, April 1966

Fabric of unblinking splendour
IMPACT by Evelyn Brooks

HEAL FABRICS

of the 1950s, shaped by American Rhythm and Blues, and Rock n' Roll, but with a distinctive British identity of their own. They recorded their first single in 1962, and achieved success from 1963 onwards, celebrated both for their music and their 'look' (neat collarless suits and shaggy mop tops). During the mid 1960s they went from strength to strength musically, although by 1965 – the year of *Help!* – the pressure of fame was beginning to tell. From this date onwards they began to explore new avenues and develop their talents as individuals, which ultimately led to the fragmentation and break-up of the group.

Similarly, 'the look' of British design in the 1960s grew out of developments during the 1950s, incorporating various stylistic influences absorbed from abroad. Crystallising around 1962, it rapidly grew in confidence, reaching a high point during the mid 1960s at the time when British pop music and Carnaby Street fashions swept the world. The title of *The Ambassador*'s 1964 feature, 'Fab Fash Pop', sums up the frenetic excitement of the period in music, fashion and design, a time of great focus, drive and creative energy. Towards the end of the decade design became more eclectic and fragmented. As designers turned increasingly to historical and ethnic sources for inspiration, the intensity of the Swinging Sixties ebbed away.

3 | When We Sat on the Floor: Furniture in the Sixties

JANE DILLON

When We Sat on the Floor: Furniture in the Sixties

JANE DILLON

T o speak of the 1960s as a breakthrough period in the context of furniture design is no exaggeration. To appreciate this I think it would perhaps be useful to know a little about what motivated designers at the time. From 1962 to 1965 I studied interior design at Manchester Regional College of Art, and from 1965 to 1968 furniture design at the Royal College of Art. The switch from interior design to specialising in furniture was significant because during that period interior design students were not allowed to specify furniture or lighting in their schemes unless it was available in this country – my reaction to this was to design the furniture myself. I disliked most of what was on offer from UK manufacturers.

During that time there were few importers of domestic furniture. The most notable were Zeev Aram, Oscar Woolands and the General Trading Company, all London based. Habitat opened in London in 1964. Within the contract market, American companies like Knoll had for a while licensed the manufacture of some of their products to Hille, before establishing Knoll International in London. Herman Miller from the United States had showrooms in London and Manchester. Scandinavia was represented by the small Finmar Ltd. shop in Knightsbridge.

It was to companies outside the United Kingdom that one turned for inspiration. We looked towards collaborations such as Arne Jacobsen's with Hansen's in Denmark; Charles and Ray Eames and Isamu Noguchi with

Figure 1. Armadio a Torre, Ettore Sottsass, 1965

Figure 2. Mail order catalogue, 1962

Herman Miller in the States under the direction of George Nelson, and indeed to Nelson himself; and to Eero Saarinen, Harry Bertoia and Florence Knoll with Knoll. In Italy there was Gio Ponti with C&B; Marco Zanuso with Arflex; and Tobia Scarpa, Achille and Pier Giacomo Castiglioni with Gavina.

These were the maestri of the Fifties whom one admired. It is their legacy above all that makes this period of furniture design so rich and that established the profession of industrial design in the furniture manufacturing industry. There was an appropriateness to their form-making that had its feet firmly planted in the new industrial reality. They were the first generation to work with manufacturing industries to produce furniture using the new materials that had become available in the period. Theirs wasn't the world of spindly legs with balls on the ends, or derivative chromed tubular metal furniture without the art of Breuer or Mies, which one found coming from many British manufacturers such as PEL in the Sixties. Their art was that of invention coupled with refined elegance of shape and form.

As a student one would keep up with what was going on outside the UK by the articles published in the Italian magazine *Domus*, edited by Gio Ponti. *Domus* was unique in that it covered fine art, architecture and applied art, each feeding off each other with excellent articles written by the most prominent arts, architects and designers of the time. George Nelson's book *Problems of Design* likewise was one of the best sources on our reading list.

Figure 3. Mail order catalogue, 1962

The interiors illustrated in *Domus* were not the watered down versions of Scandinavian furniture which had become fashionable in Britain at the end of the Fifties, the kind of furniture that left one feeling as though one was in a Hertz rent-a-car waiting room or a sauna. At the time, British furniture lacked the richness of colour and texture that had been our inheritance, so beautifully handled by the Arts and Crafts architects and designers of the late nineteenth century. The *Domus* interiors were carefully considered spaces that used the subtleties of colours and textures to create an atmosphere. Furniture and fittings were placed to enhance the space, designed to be expressed as single objects. Clutter had gone, 'applied' decoration was a dirty word; interiors were simple and often sparse.

Most people did not accept the spirit of these new interiors. In fact the average person found it difficult to stomach 'modern' and on the whole preferred old or more familiar styles. Forty years later things are beginning to change finally! But for us in the Sixties, these examples captured the best of the new spirit and fully embraced the break with tradition, without losing the richness of the best of any epoch.

The most influential architect for me during this period was Ettore Sottsass Jr. He made us realise that the things you had in your home could really change the spatial qualities of an interior. He made one rethink the role of objects and their spiritual qualities. He showed us how objects can work within the space of the interior. Sottsass developed highly figurative objects during the mid-Sixties and his influence on design thinking through his work and writings continued until the end of the Eighties. Yet it was not until his work for Memphis in 1985 that Sottsass achieved international recognition outside the design profession. *Armadio a Torre* was made for a 1966 exhibition of plastic coloured laminates. The piece in the form of an upturned ziggurat is finished in laminated plastic in graduated tones of a single colour. These laminates were given the name 'Print', and were developed by the Italian company Abet.

New plastics of all types were being developed, giving us smooth shiny surfaces, lightness and transparency. Perspex in sheet form from ICI was available for the first time and included fluorescent pink, orange and green. There was an obsession with the seamless, the smooth uninterrupted surface. The new fibres in the fashion world had freed us from stockings held up by suspenders. We now wore tights. Gone were the roll-on girdles; our bodies were free to sit

Figure 4. Eight Shades of White – One-room flat of French designer Olivier Mourgue, 1966

on the floor without discomfort.

Along with new materials for manufacture came a host of other things. Household paints were suddenly extensive in their range of colours and one did not need a professional painter to use them. For example, the colour 'white' came in various hues – something that nobody had hitherto seen other than in specialist artists' paints. The famous 'magnolia', a white that was known as off-white, was extremely popular!

It was a great period for the cross-fertilisation of ideas. The influence of Marcel Duchamp on design thinking, for those of us who understood and felt the connection, was profound. Those who felt that connection also drew inspiration from the work of the minimalist artists such as Dan Flavin, Frank Stella and Donald Judd. The Pop Art message was also a key influence. The fine artists working during this period inspired us intellectually. The shape and form

Figure 5. L'Alto Mondo Club at Rimini, 1968

of their art had a direct influence on the aesthetic that we produced. The 1968 opening of the fine art exhibition 4.Documenta in Kassel, Germany, was the first time Europe had seen gathered together in the flesh so many of the works of American artists such as Kenneth Noland, Barnet Newman and Donald Judd. The design of the L'Alto Mondo Club illustrates clearly the influence from artists of the time with its brightly coloured plastic chair shells played against their hard-edged structural supports.

It is true to say that style is a major influence on the aesthetics of a period and the manifestation of a mixture of factors. The objects with which we surround ourselves are the props of our lives. Their style, shape and form have a profound effect on our spirits and well-being. The social changes of the Sixties demanded that these props expressed this change. Whether we were into

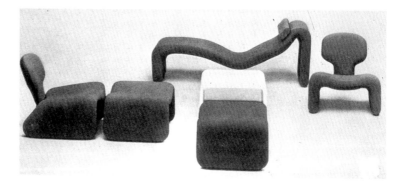

Figure 6. 'Trick', part of a series of upholstered chairs and chaises longue designed by Olivier Mourgue for Airborne, France, 1964

flower power or radical modernism, we preferred to sit on the floor, and not to be trapped by conventional furniture. Spontaneous gatherings could never happen as long as one was held in by traditional trappings such as light fittings half way up the wall on either side of the fireplace and the restrictive three-piece suite.

Olivier Mourgue was one of the first people to give new forms to upholstered furniture as seen in his series *Trick*, produced in 1964 by the French company Airborne. He took a tubular structure and bound it first in webbing, then covered this with a layer of flexible foam. This was the first time anyone had seen such pure shapes used as seating in this manner. This technique was later to be used by Pierre Paulin in his series No.577 for the Dutch company Artifort in 1966.

Tobia Scarpa's design *Bastiano* for Gavina in 1960 exploited Le Corbusier's idea of tailored loose cushions in order to make a modern sofa. This piece, combining simple, flat-sectioned wood and soft cushions and openly showing the mechanical forms of jointing, defied all conventional forms of furniture-making at the time. Its break with tradition in terms of chair construction and typology made it one of the key influences on my generation. Unconventional materials and fabrication were taken out of their normal context and used to make furniture. Two perfect examples of this are the children's chair in printed folded cardboard by Peter Murdock of 1963, designed to be flat-packed, and the inflatable armchair by De Pas, D'Urino, Lomazzi and made by Zanotta in 1969.

Perhaps the most important symbolic attack on tradition was the *Sacco* (non-chair), designed by Piero Gatti and Cesare Paolini in 1968 and produced by Zanotta in Italy. It broke with traditional design in that it had no fixed form and it allowed the user to use it however they wanted, as it moulded itself to the contours of the body. A similarly extreme breaking-away from the traditional shapes of the upholstered 'easy' chair was also made by Roger Dean in his *Sea*

Figures 7, 8. *Sacco*, designed by Piero Gatti, Cesare Paolini, Franco Teodoro and made by Zanotta, Italy, 1968

Figure 9. A Kartell advertisement of 1967 shows plastic chairs by Joe Colombo and child's chair by Marco Zanuso/Richard Sapper

Figure 10. *Selene*, designed by Vico Magistretti, 1969

Urchin during the same year. This design utilised the memory of flexible soft foam by forming a hollow sea urchin shape with a denser foam base. When a person sat on it, the hollow sea urchin form folded down on to the base forming a normal sea/back support. Both chairs would never have been possible without the development of the particular materials that they used.

Less radical upholstered furniture was also undergoing great changes due to newly available materials and the way in which the seating was designed to be used. The introduction of moulded cold-cure flexible polyurethane foams allowed designers freedom of form. There was talk afoot that by the end of the decade we would have self-skinning flexible and rigid polyurethane foam that would be able to take the place of structures that had previously been made from wood, something we take for granted when we steer our cars with moulded plastic steering wheels. There was an exciting feeling that these new materials would enable objects to be mass-produced and so be available to everyone.

By the mid-Sixties the Italian company C&B (later known as B&B) had perfected the new cold-cure moulding techniques. Mario Bellini produced the *Amanta* series, which used sophisticated glass fibre mouldings. With Tobia Scarpa's design for *Coranado*, these designs were the forerunners of what was to come in manufacturing techniques and aesthetics. Sadly, they were never to be equalled by British industry, which lagged hopelessly behind technically. *Amanta* and *Coranado* were enormously popular throughout Europe, with the exception of the United Kingdom, and were the start of what later became the most famous furniture company in Europe, Cassina. Under the directorship of Franco Cassina, the company was one of the first to realise the power of film to influence taste, and some of its furniture was used in Antonioni's and Fellini's film sets of the Sixties.

Another example of a joint collaboration with one of the new Italian manufacturers was between Kartell and two designers, Marco Zanuso and Richard Sapper. After many years of research, in 1963 they produced their first plastic injection-moulded stacking chair for children. Another chair, known as

Figure 11. 'Toio', Achille and Pier
Giacomo Castiglioni, 1962

Figure 12. From the Finnish Company
Haimi's catalogue designed by Yrjö
Kukkapuro, 1966

Selene, was also a milestone in terms of perfect refinement of structure with
immense elegance. It was designed by Vico Magistretti and produced in 1969
by Artimide. Its shape is intimately linked with its material moulding process.
The chair exemplifies the sophistication of design and manufacture coming
from Italy, unparalleled by anything in England during the Sixties.

Experimentation in manufacturing techniques for the production of
domestic lights by the Castiglioni brothers, Achille and Pier Giacomo, for
Gavina were also amazing, both in invention and form. There is a perfect
marriage between utility and the psychological demands on such objects, a
quality that is found in all the work of the brothers during this period, a quality
that makes them have lasting appeal. They too are still in production today,
sold through Flos.

It is not an exaggeration to talk of 'the furniture revolution of the Sixties'.
There was a revolution, and it fired the following decade. Industrially, the
main thrust came from Italy, and even today the Sixties' revolutionary forms
are finding their way back into contemporary design, albeit on a very superfi-
cial level.

I hope this personal sketch goes some way towards redressing the often-
voiced view that the Sixties can be summed up quite simply by blow-up pieces
of furniture and brightly-coloured crude plastic forms. It was a period of
extreme freedoms of expression, but it was also a period of great innovative
design.

4 | The Most 'In' Shops for Gear

KATE MCINTYRE

The Most 'In' Shops for Gear

KATE McINTYRE

R eporting on the Swinging London phenomenon for the *Weekend Telegraph* in November 1966, Tom Wolfe described 'The Life':

> *It all goes on within a very set style of life, based largely on clothes, music, hairdos and a ... super-cool outlook on the world. It is the style of life that makes them unique, not money, power, position, talent, intelligence ... Their clothes have come to symbolise their independence from the old idea of a life based on a succession of jobs. The hell with that.*[1]

The working-class teenagers he observed, acknowledging that they were unlikely to escape the social position into which they were born, opted to drop out of the system (while keeping their day jobs) and into alternative roles, new modes of self-presentation. The construction of identity in the act of consumption became a contemporary art form, with a generation of fashion entrepreneurs providing new kinds of shopping environments to supply innovative fashions to these 'Knights of the Codpiece Pants and Molls of the Mini Mons'.[2]

Figure 1. London shops, photographed for Ettore Sottsass, 1967. (Photo courtesy Jane Dillon)

Figure 2. Carnaby Street in 1968. (*The Guardian*, photographer Eric Wadsworth)

1. 'Tom Wolfe's Britain 3 – The Noonday Underground', *Weekend Telegraph*, 11 November 1966, p.10.

2. ibid, p.9.

Collaboration between a middle class art student and her eccentric upper-class boyfriend over ten years earlier had triggered a rash of London boutiques. Mary Quant and Alexander Plunket Greene (along with their lawyer/photographer partner Archie McNairn) opened Bazaar above the eponymous Alexander's basement restaurant on the King's Road in November 1955. It was a very Chelsea Set thing to do, 'a kind of permanently running cocktail party'.[3] The shop front, in essence the same as those of myriad 1950s 'Can I help you Madam?' ladies-wear shops that dressed young women like their mothers, was subverted by the use of window tableaux of mannequins in kooky poses, wearing Quant's stylised versions of art school, beat-inspired, looks. The displays changed frequently and were noted for their surrealist wit – in one a mannequin walked a lobster on a long gold leash.[4] Beneath the banner 'Bazaar', invoking the exoticism of the Souk, was the Quant daisy logo that would become the emblem of Swinging London and an internationally recognised brand by 1966.

To wear Quant was to express rebellion against the adult establishment while conspicuously displaying membership of a social elite, whose parameters were, ostensibly, defined by youth, beauty, wit or talent rather than class. The formula was hugely successful and in 1957 a second Bazaar opened on Knightsbridge Green, designed by another member of the Set – Bryanston old boy Terence Conran – and later a third in Bond Street. These boutiques were merely a means to an end – the real money lay in mass-production. In 1962 Quant signed deals with the us store J.C. Penney, Butterick Patterns and Puritan Fashions, and started the wholesale Ginger Group a year later. The King's Road Bazaar closed in 1968, the other two soon after. However, Quant proved that mass-produced fashion did not have to be just couture knock offs – that young designers could provide what the young consumer wanted.

What Quant did for womenswear, John Stephen did for menswear, opening His Clothes, the first of ten Carnaby Street boutiques, in neighbouring Beak Street in 1959. He was building on the success of Vince in Newburgh Street, Bill Green's chic men's outfitters established in 1954 for a mainly gay clientele that had gained a number of heterosexual celebrity customers including Peter Sellers. While the original Mods, described by George Melly as 'a very small group of working class boys who formed a small totally committed little mutual admiration society totally devoted to clothes, working class dandies, dedicated followers of fashion',[5] used tailors and shoemakers to kit themselves out; as the style spread the need for suitable readymade fashion fuelled the Carnaby Street boom. Stephen supplied a winning combination of Italian styling and pop design to a growing sector of young male consumers, who, without being overtly homosexual, were narcissists to a man. As Nik Cohn pointed out, 'every time you passed a John Stephen window there was something new and loud in it, and when you counted your money you found you could afford it.'[6] Soon there were imitators such as Donis and and by 1966 Carnaby Street, bedecked with Union Jacks, became a tacky tourist trap rather than a Mecca for Modernists.

The department stores, whose staid middle-aged buyers maintained conservative attitudes based on the haute couture seasons, eventually set up their own in-store boutiques in response to the success of these young entrepreneurs in the King's Road and Carnaby Street. While Harrods did not open 'Way-In' until 1966, Woolands, next door to Harvey Nichols in Knightsbridge, launched 21 Shop on 15 September 1961 in tandem with a 15-page spread in *Vogue*. Again it was Conran who designed the interior and the buyers, Vanessa Denza and Maggie Arkell, were young, in their early twenties. They carried Mary Quant and supported several new designers including Jean Muir. Stock changed completely fifteen times a year and best selling designs were swiftly re-supplied by the factory at unprecedented rates, up to 1,000 garments a week. Denza followed her instincts, working with the designers and the manufactur-

3. Mary Quant, *Quant by Quant*, London, Cassell, 1966, p.45.

4. Janet Ozzard 'Retailing in the 1960s: The Phenomenon of the Boutique', *Textile and Text*, Vol.12, No.3, 1990, p.7.

5. George Melly, *Revolt into Style*, Oxford, 1970, p.168.

6. Nik Cohn, *Today there are no Gentlemen*, London, Weidenfeld & Nicolson, 1971, p.66.

ers to create clothes at the right price points. 'When I said that I thought we would achieve these figures everybody said I was mad and I was completely right. It was like so much was pent up and hadn't happened.'[7] By the time Denza left in 1964, another five 21 Shops had been opened in Debenhams stores around the country, the buying tailored for each location. Although the shops were highly successful Denza recognised that they posed a threat to the antiquated systems and retailing approaches of the Debenham management. Woolands was eventually sold and 'everything that was good in it' was moved over to Harvey Nichols.

Barbara Hulanicki, a fashion illustrator who sketched at the Paris collections in the late fifties and early sixties, was well aware of the stasis in Paris and London fashions, both couture and ready to wear. She found it virtually impossible to find suitable clothes, even Quant's 'deb's clothes' were 'graded enormous' and were too expensive for the average teenage girl who wanted style, but at the right price.[8] With a basic training in fine art and fashion from Brighton Art School but without the financial backing enjoyed by Quant (who had launched Bazaar with a £5,000 inherited by Plunket Greene plus £5,000 from Archie McNairn) Hulanicki and her husband Stephen Fitz-Simon went into business as Biba's Postal Boutique in 1963. Courtesy of Hulanicki's contacts in the fashion press, a feature in the *Daily Mirror* in May 1964 generated huge sales and enough money to launch their own boutique, Biba's, in a chemist's shop at 87 Abingdon Road, Kensington.

In the wake of Bazaar the rag trade had opened up a string of 'space age' boutiques along the King's Road. Harry Feingold of Della Amber had commissioned the architects Garnett, Cloughley, Blakemore to produce 'modern' and 'exciting' interiors for Just Looking, I Spy, Stop the Shop (a revolving shop) and

7. Vanessa Denza, interview with author, London, 23 February 1994.

8. Barbara Hulanicki, and Stephen Fitz-Simon, interview with author, Miami South Beach, Florida, 12 February 1994.

Figure 3. Just Looking, King's Road, Chelsea. Garnett, Cloughley, Blakemore. Exterior shot of futuristic polished stainless stell façade with 'peephole' window/entrance arches. With the absence of the usual panel behind the mannequins, the dark interior is visible. Signage in 'computer writing'. All very James Bond. (Photo courtesy Patrick Garnett)

Figure 4. Interior of the Just Looking, King's Road, Chelsea. Garnett, Cloughley, Blakemore. The 'total design' concept incorporates racking, shelves, and handles in GCB stock-in-trade futuristic polished stainless steel, mirror, Perspex and glass. (Photo courtesy Patrick Garnett)

Gypsy. The results were highly polished stainless steel and mirror clad 'space capsules'.[9] This type of futuristic interior was inspired by the Smithsons' 1955 'House of the Future', a series of interchangeable chrome trimmed plastic capsule rooms, and coincided with Courrège's Space Age couture collection of 1964. The televised Space Race pervaded popular consciousness and contemporary design reflected the fascination with space fact and space fiction until the end of the decade. When the King's Road Bazaar closed in 1968, Garnett, Cloughley, Blakemore transformed it into the Markham Pharmacy and in 1969 they used a similar futuristic style in the Chelsea Drugstore and the Albrizzi showroom in Sloane Square.

Space Age imagery was not at all what Hulanicki had in mind for Biba's. She wanted to recreate the interior of an authentic Parisian boutique and chose to retain the peeling blue paint and the remains of the original name on the shop's fascia. Biba's traded for two years in a rather obscure location without a name over the door – the appeal lay in the fact that the clientèle were 'in with the in-crowd'. Hulanicki sought mystery and exoticism over shiny futurism. The clothing on sale was simple mini-Mod but with the essential Biba retro hallmarks – tight high armholes, high-buttoned necklines and puff sleeves. The décor was pure retro-chic: the black and white floor tiles copied from the Polish court scene in *Ivan the Terrible*, the walls painted dark blue, and the floor-to-ceiling windows on two sides curtained in plum and navy William Morris print to keep out the light and maintain the requisite darkness that evoked the French 'discothèque'. Minimal lighting came from two borrowed bronze lamps with black shades – the antithesis of the High Street Fashion shops with their fluorescent strip and spot lighting. Parlour palms were placed in Victorian jardinières; clothes were displayed on second-hand bentwood hat stands rather than the circular chrome rails used in Just Looking. Hulanicki was an avid collector of Victoriana and Art Nouveau she used to furnish her own flat. In an interview in 1966 she summed up her eclectic personal taste: 'I love old things. Modern things are so cold. I need things that have lived.'[10] The whole point of the designer-owned boutique was that it reflected the personal aesthetic of its owner who was often present in the shop. The close relationship between consumer and producer was key to the success of these ventures. The clients' own sense of individuality, the way in which they put the clothes together to create their own look, was as important as the designer's vision and often influenced it.

Abingdon Road opened in the year that *Ready Steady Go*, a new youth music programme, was first broadcast. Cathy McGowan would wear Biba on the show one week, Tuffin and Foale or Sonia Rykiel for Laura, imported by James Wedge and Pat Booth for their boutique Top Gear, the next. McGowan was the epitome of the London 'dolly' and was slavishly copied by the television audience, generating an unheard of 'new outfit a week' buying cycle. Her high-profile endorsement ensured Biba's immediate success. In the chaos of the dark communal changing room some shoplifting was inevitable. Sometimes a pile of non-Biba clothes would be discovered – their owner having walked out of the shop in a new outfit and left her own clothes behind.

As Bibas became more successful Hulanicki came into contact with young designers such as Julie Hodgess, a recent Royal College of Art textiles graduate who first designed a black and gold Art Nouveau-inspired wallpaper for the shop in 1965, followed up by prints for the clothes. Hodgess lived in a Notting Hill Gate bedsit close to Portobello Road, which was starting to gain a reputation as an antiques market. I was Lord Kitchener's Valet offered a range of Sgt. Pepper-type military jackets, original Victorian lighting was available from the stall of an out of work actor, Christopher Wray, and Dodo Designs on Westbourne Grove stocked original and reproduction enamel signs, evoking the early days of consumerism before large scale mass-production threatened

Figure 5. Interior of Abingdon Road Biba, 1965, wallpaper by Julie Hodgess. (Photo courtesy Julie Hodgess, photographer unknown)

9. Patrick Garnett, interview with author, London, 5 November 1993.

10. 'Take a Look at this New Face, It Belongs to 1966', *Daily Telegraph*, 27 October 1966, quoted in J. Harris, S. Hyde and G. Smith, *1966 and All That*, London, Trefoil Books, 1986, p.84.

individuality and authenticity. Contemporary interiors combined modern design with nostalgic elements, traditional, handcrafted objects from an idealised past or from the pre-industrial (Mediterranean) countryside were sought after to humanise the relentlessly modern interior. Terence Conran's 'shop for switched-on people',[11] Habitat, also opened in 1964 supplying the 'progressive middle-classes' with an eclectic mix of reproduction Victoriana, French traditional cookware, 'Victorian Campaign chest[s] in teak or oak', 'Trad. French salad bowls', white porcelain, and gaudy enamel mugs. Nineteenth-century bentwood chairs were stacked warehouse style alongside contemporary designs and mass-produced reproductions of Modern Movement classics.[12]

In March 1966 Biba moved to new premises in Kensington Church Street with 1,100 square feet of selling space, four times that of Abingdon Road. Hulanicki retained the original 'Home and Colonial' mahogany shelving and counters, which were complemented with bargains from the Furniture Cave off Praed Street in Paddington: antique gilt mirrors for less than £30, Victorian wardrobes, £5 china jardinières for the parlour palms. The floor was again tiled in black and white; clothes were hung on the same bentwood hat stands and trousers displayed on Victorian wooden towel rails. Feather boas, dyed in bright colours to match the clothes, were introduced as decorations and soon became standard Biba stock. A friend of Julie Hodgess, Anthony Little, was brought in to paint the word Biba above the shop and to black out the windows to reduce the light level in the shop. Hodgess describes how Hulanicki wanted '… a shopfront which was slightly secretive, with an Art Nouveau symbol in the centre of it which was open and the rest of it very decorative, very much like their logo, it was all taken from that same thing.'[13]

On each window Little left a peephole outlined in gold and 'surrounded by Art Nouveau squiggles' which became the new Biba logo. The peepholes

Figure 6. Anthony Little looks through his window for Church Street Biba, 1966. (Photo courtesy Rosie Young, photographer unknown)

11. Habitat press release, cited by Fiona McCarthy, *British Design since 1880*, London, Lund Humphries, 1982, p.156.

12. Instore catalogue, Habitat, 1964, courtesy of Ben Weaver.

13. Julie Hodgess, interview with author, London, 10 January 1994.

Figure 7. Kim Willott (sales assistant) in Church Street Biba, *c.*1966. (Photo courtesy Kim Willott, photographer unknown)

proved to be an irresistible draw to passers by; Hulanicki's strategy of secrecy was successful to the extent that each morning the sales girls would have to remove the marks left by the noses of those that peered in. The window seats inside the shop were scattered with multicoloured velvet cushions, a Julie Hodgess trademark, on which customers or bored husbands could relax. This seating facility, abandoned by retailers who wanted a throughput of custom-ers, was a standard feature of all Biba shops. While the shopfront of Bazaar had made innovative use of display mannequins, it retained the traditional store window approach with a window display separated from the rest of the shop by a backdrop. Hulanicki abandoned this concept altogether. There was no need to display examples of the merchandise available inside the store to the outside world. Hulanicki never used mannequins, either in the windows of her stores or inside.

Ian Culow and Maz Murray also adopted the strategy of luring in the curi-ous customer with a similar decorative painted shopfront for Gandalf's Garden, a 'head-shop' that stocked hippy clothing, wholefoods, alternative litera-ture and handcrafted objects. Poster artist Nigel Waymouth used the same tactics for the window of Granny Takes a Trip at World's End on the King's Road, which at one point featured a car emerging from a blank wall. The front-age changed frequently while inside the stock moved from vintage beaded dresses and blazers to original designs by partners Waymouth, Shelagh York and John Pearse.[14] The retailing approach was elitist, grounded in the New Aristocrat snobbery, and the clothing expensive. Granny's, along with John Critall's Dandie Fashions on the King's Road and Michael Rainey and Jane Ormsby-Gore's Hung on You in Cale Street, Chelsea, formed an elite alterna-tive to the more populist Carnaby Street boutiques.

The interior of the Church Street Biba appeared in a series of photographs taken by Ettore Sottsass Jr. under the title 'Whipped Cream Memoirs' in *Domus* for January 1967. Lettering by the artist Derek Boshier for Pauline Fordham's boutique Palisades on Carnaby Street featured in the same photo-graphic essay celebrating the visual style of Swinging London. However, the interiors of the two boutiques could not have been more different. While Fordham went the masculine Pop Art route with changing room curtains printed with images of the Union Jack and the Stars and Stripes,[15] the overall effect of the Biba interior was that of a demi-mondaine's boudoir, feminine and decadent. Hulanicki wanted to 'transform the "new changing room into a bordello"' with red walls and carpet, and Julie Hodgess was commissioned to produce a new wallpaper in red, maroon and gold. The changing room was in the basement and Hodgess designed a 'cut out blockboard staircase with Art Nouveau details' which was painted in 'strong bright colours – magenta and orange' to match the wallpaper.[16] In an *Evening Standard* Home Page feature in August 1966, Hodgess compared her wallpaper designs for Church Street to the Beardsley prints that were on display at the V&A that summer. 'Julie did a fantabulous art nouveau design in red, aubergine and gold for the London shop and a gold on brown one for the Brighton shop. "Like Aubrey Beardsley jungles" she calls them'.[17]

Biba customers remember Church Street as 'the best Biba shop – all gloom, mirrors and palms', 'a shadowy shop with hat stands with bright things dan-gling from them.'[18] The appeal lay in the feeling that you entered 'a dark and glittering cave of affordable treasure'[19] and came out with a bargain. A little money went a long way in Biba, as one customer remembers: 'Everything was such good fun. So much money to spend on clothes'.[20] The Biba consumer was classless, the more money she had, the more outfits she would buy. It was not a question of going elsewhere – it had to be Biba. Biba was now literally 'on the map' that accompanied the *Time Magazine* article on Swinging London in April 1966, which declared: 'the most In shop for gear is Biba's boutique ... which is the most scene for the switched on dolly-bird.' Biba was definitely 'in' and 'stars and would-be stars ... flocked to the shop' whether it was to buy a new dress for a Saturday evening date or to appear on TV or in a movie.[21] Julie Christie bought clothes to wear in the 1965 movie *Darling* from Abingdon Road, Sonny and Cher, Cilla Black, Sandie Shaw, Chrissie Shrimpton, Mia Far-row, Brigitte Bardot, Marianne Faithful, Barbara Streisand, Yoko Ono and Samantha Eggar, as well as Twiggy, were all early high-profile Biba customers.

In 1969 Biba relocated to even larger premises on Kensington High Street. The interior decoration reflected a progression through time, from Art Nouveau towards Art Deco, a shift that was reflected in the evolving taste of the London design cognoscenti. Hulanicki claimed that the progression in retro styles for her stores rose out of a desire to conserve the prevailing period decor of the buildings that they were in:

Although Biba [began] as Art Nouveau, we never wished to ruin the original style of any premises. If the mouldings were Deco, they would stay

14. Nigel Waymouth, quoted in Jonathon Green, *Days in the Life*, London, Heinemann, 1988, p.220.

15. Penny Sparke, *Theory and Design in the Age of Pop*, unpublished PhD Thesis, University of Brighton, 1975, p.146.

16. Julie Hodgess, interview with author, London, 10 January 1994.

17. Barbara Anne Taylor, 'Home Page', *Evening Standard*, Thursday 18 August 1966.

18. Quoted in Caroline Imlah, *Biba: The Label, The Lifestyle, The Look*, Exhibition Catalogue, Newcastle, Laing Art Gallery, 1993.

19. Georgina Howell, *Sultans of Style*, London, Ebury Press, 1990, p.xv.

20. Mrs Yeats, quoted in Jemma Cooper, *Bring Out Your Biba*, extracts from interviews (October 1992) with lenders to the exhibition *Biba: The Label, The Lifestyle, The Look*, Laing Art Gallery Archives.

21. Barbara Hulanicki, *From A to Biba*, London, Comet, 1983, p.79.

*Deco. Had we moved into a fifties building I would not have altered its
character.*[22]

The site did not have any immediately obvious period appeal, having been
modernised for use as a carpet showroom by Cyril Lord. The double fronted
window was plate glass, and inside the showroom itself was an anonymous,
streamlined shell. As work started an elegant mezzanine emerged from a
boxed-in office and a curving period stair rail from the panelled stairs leading
down to the basement. Around the walls of the ground floor were a series of
1920s Egyptian-topped columns that, sprayed gold, served as a starting point
for Hodgess's design for the wallpaper frieze. The motifs in the frieze have been
referred to as 'Art Deco Egyptian-revival' but the design actually stems from
examples of Egyptian Ornament in Owen Jones's *Grammar of Ornament*,
which Hodgess had inherited from her architect father.

Hulanicki and Hodgess's views on the retailing environment coincided.
Although the new shop was to be spacious and elegant, they did not want it to
be intimidating, they wanted a frontage that would 'funnel people in' to the
new Biba.[23] Hodgess overlaid the design of a bow fronted Victorian shopfront
at 61 Westbourne Grove, on the corner of Kensington Gardens Square, on to
the original Cyril Lord façade. She and her team produced detailed architectural drawings for the whole project and were responsible for the design of the
ground floor.

The inclusion of a household department reflected consumer demand –
the Biba customer was either leaving home to move into a shared flat or taking the next step: getting married, setting up home and having children. Habitat had proved there was a market, and Hulanicki wanted to offer 'household
goods that worked with Art Nouveau, Victorian or Edwardian furniture'.[24] A
new line of Biba menswear was displayed in the basement, designed by
Anthony Little; more expensive, sophisticated evening wear and leather were
on the mezzanine, designed by Hulanicki herself; below this was a children's
department designed by a new young team, Whitmore-Thomas. The retail
environment was 'growing up' with the Biba customer.

The black and white tiled floor that had been a keynote at Church Street
and Abingdon Road was replaced with elegant marble to create a feeling of
space. Carved wood panelling and pillars, acquired at auction along with
stained glass windows for £100 from the recently demolished St Paul's School,
were used to refurbish the mezzanine and the basement. 'Shelving units that
looked like giant dressers' were requested by Hulanicki and designed by
Hodgess and her team to display bags and shoes. At the front of the shop one
large display unit was installed to house the newly launched line of Biba cosmetics.

In the basement Anthony Little used the stained glass from St Paul's and his
own wallpaper designs to create a conservatory, with an assortment of Victorian pub tables and ceramic wash bowls used to display the merchandise. The
price of bentwood hat stands having escalated to £15 with demand, the
Hulanicki bought new Czechoslovakian imports. Two changing rooms were
provided to accommodate the growing Saturday crowds, the main changing
room with floor to ceiling mirrors, the smaller one, with classic 'film star'
changing room mirrors surrounded by light bulbs.

Hulanicki decorated the mezzanine area in pale pink with a cream carpet
and velvet chaises longues. Beneath it was the children's department for which
Whitmore-Thomas were briefed to create a giant doll's house for the display of
the clothes and as a play area for the children. The whole Kensington High
Street project was completed in 6 weeks, from late July to September 1969.[25]

As Hulanicki diversified her product range a strong graphic style was required to avoid fragmentation of the Biba identity. Anthony Little's logo in
black and gold was used on packaging and carrier bags in Church Street and

22. ibid, p.112.

23. Julie Hodgess, interview with author,
London, 10 January 1994.

24. Hulanicki, *op.cit*, p.113.

25. Steve Thomas, interview with author,
London, 25 November 1993.

the short-lived 'satellite' Biba boutiques in Brighton and Zermatt. John McConnell worked with Hulanicki on mail order catalogues in 1968 and 1969, retaining the Art Nouveau feel in his use of a Celtic woodblock design combined with a nineteenth century commercial typeface, Arnold Bocklin in a new Biba logo. This 'fat' Celtic logo was used on the mail order catalogues and packaging and in 1970 McConnell redrew a 'thin' Biba alphabet. A new logo comprising the word Biba in the new typeface set underneath only one block of the Celtic design had a more streamlined feel to it, reflecting the move towards Art Deco that began in the High Street Kensington store. This logo was first used on the final Biba catalogue in summer 1969 and became the logo for the Biba cosmetics range.

Eventually the label became the product with Biba tights, Biba baked beans packaged in distinctive black and gold retro designs. Each of the five floors of the final Biba in the huge 1930s Derry & Toms department store that opened in 1973 had individual logo, labels and packaging designed by Steve Thomas, whose team was responsible for the refit. In total fifteen different logos were used. However, Big Biba foundered as Hulanicki lost creative control. In order to make the move into Kensington High Street, Biba had been refinanced and become a Limited Company with Fitz-Simon and Hulanicki holding just 25% of the shares. Biba failed within six months of the installation of an all-male administration by majority shareholders Dorothy Perkins/British Land – a move that prompted Hulanicki to walk out on her creation. The site was sold to Marks and Spencers, the epitome of the mediocrity that Biba had fought against.

The designer-owned boutiques of the sixties were outlived by their 'rag-

Figure 8. Big Biba newspaper distributed at launch in 1973. Courtesy Steve Thomas. (Kate McIntyre)

Figure 9. Biba catalogue 1968, cover and logo by John McConnell. (Kate McIntyre)

Figure 10. Granny Takes A Trip, King's Road, in 1969

Figure 11. Biba tights, *c*.1973. Logo by Steve Thomas. Photo courtesy Laing Art Gallery

trade' equivalents, Way-In, Chelsea Girl, and Miss Selfridge. Bazaar closed as Quant moved into mass-production, Granny Takes a Trip was sold on in 1969 as Nigel Waymouth tired of the novelty. Biba just survived into the recession-hit seventies. The success of the boutique relied on the total design of what Peter York calls 'a saturated personal aesthetic'[26] and could not survive the transition into a department store. The auction of the contents of Big Biba in 1975 marked the very end of an era.

26. Peter York, presentation at the V&A/RCA MA History of Design course, Victoria and Albert Museum, 13th January 1994.

5 | The Space Between

PETER SMITHSON

The Space Between

PETER SMITHSON

I gave an interview to a student from Bath who had made an interpretation of the work in Urbino. Towards the end of her dissertation, she said, 'In the time of massive developments there is no consideration of the in-betweens.' And, of course, it instantly flashes into one's mind that the palace of Duke Federico Montefelto is an absolutely massive megastructure, and the size of the Palazzo Ducale in relation to Urbino at that time is very similar to the size of the shopping-hypermarket against the pygmy dwellings which frequently surround them. The quality of such a structure and its in-betweens is completely dependent on the quality of the architect.

The Sixties for us personally was the beginning of the discovery and investigation of the space between. In 1959 I designed a wallpaper in which the base image is ambiguous – is it a centaur or a man on a horse? But with it being a wallpaper in strips the relationship between the images which occur is random. Therefore the quality of the image is the space between and not the object.

In the Fifties also we did the basic work (in 1955–1956) on *The Heroic Period of Modern Architecture*.[1] The introduction states:

> *The documents have been photographed and the collection reviewed as a whole and edited during 1965 with the help of Christopher Woodward.*[2]
>
> *A few pieces of text have been inserted at this stage which, it is hoped, will*

Figure 1. The Farnsworth House, Plaino, Illinois; Mies van der Rohe, 1945–50. Column between the upper (house) and lower (landing) platforms. (P.S., September 1984)

Figure 2. Two wallpapers by Peter Smithson from the Palladio Magnus range, no.44440, 'Digitus', 1959. (Walter Hoyle, 1959; *Interior Design*)

1. Alison and Peter Smithson, 'The Heroic Period of Modern Architecture', in *Architectural Design*, vol.35, no.12, December 1965, reprinted Thames and Hudson 1981.

2. Christopher Woodward was at that time working in our office.

3. Note from 2002: This has turned out to be, for the normality of building, completely wrong. The new buildings along the m4 to the airport, for example, are 'object buildings', much worse than can be imagined.

Figure 3. The Economist Building, St James's Street, London; Alison and Peter Smithson, 1959–64. 'Three men on the Plaza', looking towards Brook's Club in St James's Street. (Michael Carapetian, 1964)

illuminate the pattern of the choice of the material.' Then comes the critical bit. *'We have had one afterthought, and that is that this is probably the last collection of its kind. The next collection in forty years' time of the architecture of our own period will be quite different for it will not record* buildings, *but built-places, and the documents will be mostly air views, sequential photographs, and system explanations. Our documents* [– the documents of the Heroic Period –] *are still very much like those of Bannister Fletcher on the Italian Renaissance* [they are documents of objects, buildings as objects].

Now, that was December 1965. It placed the beginning and end of the Heroic Period as 1922–29, so that the centre of that period was, say, 1925. That was forty years forward and one felt justified that enough time had elapsed to select the images that showed the flow of the ideas. Forty years from 1965 brings you to 2005, when in my view the new collection of the critical documents of our period will be quite different and they will be documents concerning the space between.[3]

The Economist Building was designed in 1959 and completed in 1964. The first edition of the paper from the new address came out on 6 June 1964. I remember it because 6 June was D-Day. So the Economist also, like the publication of this Heroic Period document, comes in the middle of the period that the Twentieth Century Society is interested in. Some photographs of the buildings there seem to me to catch the nature of the space between. The most asked-for photograph of The Economist is this one taken by Michael Carapetian, and because of the nature of the empooling of the space, those people walking through it are particularly vivid. You can't photograph space, so anything that I have as slides or as black and white photographs is a simulacrum for experience. The buildings are making the space, but the palpability of the space is separate from the palpability of the building.

Why the Economist works with space is because it was perceived that buildings are surrounded by a spatial energy field. When you have a long rectangular building you have a long rectangular energy field. Squarish-in-plan buildings have an ability to mesh in with the existing energy fields. Therefore, the space is a combination of the energy of what is existing and what you're putting in it. It is not that the buildings look good together, but that the spaces built in aggregate have a joint spatial energy.

That is difficult to think about and difficult to accept, so that when you say that the building's first duty is to the fabric of which it forms part, is not that duty to re-energise the existing spatial energy? We are coming into a slightly metaphysical notion of architecture, when we embark on this idea.

I must continue with the difficult bit.

In 1963 I first became dimly aware of a metaphysical notion of space in a building by Mies van der Rohe when on a visit to the Afrikanischestrasse in Berlin which was built in 1926–27. Again, I have to say that you can't photograph what I experienced. I felt then that the distance between the road and the buildings was critical to the Afrikanischestrasse. It just looks like a terribly tedious block of pre-war modern housing in photographs: it is not like that in real life to me!

And you could say that it is customary to talk about Mies van der Rohe in

Figure 4. Demonstrators resting on The Economist Building steps up from St James's Street. (P.S., 23 October 1983)

Figure 5. Municipal Housing in the Afrikanischestrasse, Berlin; Mies van der Rohe, 1926–27. View from the street. (P.S., March 1963)

51

the sense of his mastery over proportion. But proportion is the wrong word: proportion implies geometric relationships, whereas I believe what is magical in Mies van der Rohe is the consonance of things in their actuality not in their geometries. That quality in this building is striking. It is just plain cement render. The cement render looks wonderful. The very cementness of it is what is in the proportion. When we talk about Mies's proportion, we are not talking about as they were made in a drawing, but as they hit you in their actual presence.

This was a glimmering of what I later perceived as something that Mies van der Rohe can do which you can barely talk about, and that is that the space

Figure 6. The Neue Nationalgalerie, Berlin; Mies van der Rohe, 1962–68. It has been said that in certain works of Mies van der Rohe that 'the space without is within'; here in Berlin, in the late 1990s, in spite of later buildings coming close the sense of the control of the 'space without' is held. (P.S., 1967)

without is contained within. The building lays down its spaces around it, whether or not there is actual physical space, the sense of the exterior space is there in the building. And this is a thing so difficult to struggle for. Eighteen aspects of the play between existing circumstance and the new building on the Economist were worked for. But why it works is not because of those eighteen things; there are additional factors that come into it, which were not imagined into it.

To continue to focus on the space-without-within of Mies van der Rohe. The Neue Nationalgalerie in Berlin has been surrounded by further new buildings and yet one becomes increasingly conscious of its spatial control. The spatial control can be corrupted by subsequent buildings but it still remains. At that point, you realise that you are dealing with a concept which you can't really handle. Therefore, all I can do is be like the traditional art historian who says the function of the art historian is to make a map, that is, to get you to the building. That is also my function.

However, with Mies this space-without-within is not always present. At the Farnsworth House there is first the landing platform, then the house platform: a kind of Mississippi levée – one step and then another step above a potentially floodable ground. The space here is entirely literal, not of this metaphysical sort I am talking about. The Farnsworth House was designed in 1945–9 which is quite astonishing, and the Eames House is 1949, and Aalto's Säynätsalo Town Hall is 1949; that is, all the critical things in my lifetime happened in 1949, like all the critical things in the first Heroic Period happened in 1925.

For the historian, this space-between notion produces two problems of assessment. If the insertion of the new thing with these spatial characteristics

improves the circumstance by the interlock of the spaces with the existing spaces, it produces a wholly new criteria of assessment: you are not saying this is a beautiful object, you are saying in what way does it enhance the circumstance. And from that is an even more shattering notion and that is, if you are considering the conservation of a building with these spatial characteristics, it is no good saying put a conservation order on the building because it is not in the building, it is in the space. We have to be conscious of spaces. To give a crude example: Enric Miralles telephoned me one evening and said 'what is the width of the Campo in Siena?' And I said, it could be between 300m and 500m, and I then rushed about trying to find a plan with a scale on it, so that I could scale it and ring him back. And I had misjudged the dimension by a factor of one hundred percent.

If it is true that a book of our period, 60s, 70s, 80s, 90s, in forty years time will be one of recording spaces, there will be a combination of existing spaces and old spaces, and that feeds on to the problem of conservation. We have become

Figure 7. The Eames' House, Santa Monica, California; Charles and Ray Eames, 1949. The house and the studio beyond, seen from the 'meadow' through the line of the eucalyptus trees. The space – between trees and house is critical. (P.S., November 1978)

Figure 8. Lever House, New York; Skidmore, Owings and Merrill, 1952. To the left is the Racquet Club, McKim, Mead and White; right, an office building by Emery Roth. (P.S., 1957)

accustomed to saying that it is no good keeping that one building, because unless the street is there the building loses meaning. One of the critical inputs into The Economist Building was seeing the Lever House 1948–51 which, by ignoring the energy of Fifth Avenue, was very destructive. Therefore, that was a kind of negative signpost, that is not a way forward. Fifth Avenue is the thing with the rich spatial energy, and the new thing has got to give to that richness something. Or, if it is terrible, the reverse, if you see what I mean. If it is a terrible street, the building has to have a destructive energy to the terribleness or the re-organisation of the space, so that it works. Following that line of thought, you end up with problems you haven't really properly thought about, but know intuitively you have to act on.

So I think I have to leave you with the problems I haven't properly thought about, and thank you for giving me the chance of putting the notes together of what realisations happened to us in the Sixties.

6 | White Light/White Heat: Rebuilding England's Provincial Towns and Cities in the Sixties

ELAIN HARWOOD

White Light/White Heat: Rebuilding England's Provincial Towns and Cities in the Sixties

ELAIN HARWOOD

W
e are beginning again to appreciate the icon buildings of the 1960s: the new universities and the additions made at Oxford and Cambridge, the London landmarks such as the Economist Building and the Brunswick Centre. But the Sixties were about much more. Most towns and cities, especially northern ones, were totally transformed by new shopping and housing schemes. After only a very few years many of these slid out of favour, were neglected and have been blamed for countless social ills. Only by unscrambling the conditions that produced the towers and underpasses can we begin to understand how at the time they symbolised what superficially seemed a brighter new age.

The northern city is a quintessentially nineteenth-century foundation. There may be an old core, a parish church extended and upgraded to cathedral status with a small close of Georgian houses in its shadow, but the layout is largely defined by railway lines and industry, and is Victorian. In 1960 Ian Nairn compared northern cities with those of America: a commercial core ringed by entirely separate areas of housing, with none of the social integration historically found in London. 'Corporation Street in Birmingham or Piccadilly in Manchester were never intended to be lived in: ... Each has a centre surrounded by a ring of blight, the exact pattern of Chicago and all other nineteenth-century American cities. Our first experiment in trying to equate material progress with true progress has blown up in our faces – a metaphorical explosion assisted in varying degrees by the real explosions of 1940–1.'[1]

Neither the people nor the conditions behind the Sixties urban transformation were young, but had grown up together in the war. Wartime devastation had left parts of English cities bare, but with the exceptions of Coventry, Plymouth and Hull city centres had been hit in a piecemeal way, and Newcastle and Nottingham were barely touched. The damage was enough, however, to suggest where slum clearance and redevelopment might continue. Moreover, a generation of councillors and planners had seen how comprehensive strategies had won Britain the war, and they had no reservations about using such powers in peacetime. When Donald Gibson produced his redevelopment proposals for Coventry in February 1941 the powers of acquiring land to realise the scheme did not exist. But this deficiency had been anticipated by the Barlow Report of 1940, and Town and Country Planning Acts in 1943 and 1944 made land purchases much easier than before (and than they were to become in the Fifties and Sixties).[2] Following the lead of London and Hull, by the end of the war every major town and city, and some predominantly rural areas such as the Durham coalfields, were producing 'plans', which formed the basis under the 1947 Town and Country Planning Act for local policies. Local authority powers were transformed by the nationalisation of local services and the new provisions for land utilisation and compulsory purchase. Many schemes that came to fruition only in the 1960s had their origins in these idealised visions from the last years of the war.

But in between also came a more spontaneous response to the new

Figure 1. CIS Building, Manchester. Burnet, Tait and Partners, 1959–62. (All photos Elain Harwood)

1. Ian Nairn, 'Birmingham: Liverpool: Manchester', in *Architectural Review*, vol.187, no.762, August 1960, p.111.

2. John Holliday, *City Centre Redevelopment*, London, Charles Knight and Co., 1973, pp.5–6.

3. J.M. Richards, 'Buildings of the Year: 1954', in *Architects' Journal*, vol.121, no.3125, 20 January 1955, p.86.

4. *Built Environment*, vol.1, no.10, October 1972, p.448.

5. Zita Adamson, *Sam Chippindale, Shopping Centre Pioneer*, Saltaire, Sam Chippindale Foundation, 1993, p.13.

consumer age. As J.M. Richards recognised, 'Coventry is almost unique in having made a plan after the bombing and (subject to minor changes) carried it through with determination, while other bombed cities were allowing *laisser-faire* gradually to take charge.'[3] Behind this casual statement lurked the activities of a new kind of property developer, different to his forebears in his scale of operation, mobilisation, large resources and with an increasingly sophisticated credit system he could marry to the favourable economic climate. Harold Samuel, Joe and David Levy, Joe Littman, Charles Clore and Felix Fenston had worked in the Thirties as London estate agents, and by 1945 they had cheaply acquired bomb sites of incredible potential. As Lord Holford put it, 'the developer is a new social phenomenon, a middleman, often starting with nothing and continually putting out antennae to any scent of putting together a site and a client … There is a way of life with a technique of promises and threats. For example, Charlie Clore promising Liverpool a new civic centre and bus station in return for a slice of development land, on the one hand, and Shell threatening the LCC on another. "One million sq ft or we move to the continent."'[4]

The single largest reason for the delay of over twenty years was the restrictions caused by the licensing of building works to control materials in short supply, primarily steel and timber, and limit inflation. These controls were aimed to target resources towards schools, houses and industry, in greatest need after the war, and were actually tightened in 1947–8 following the withdrawal of American lend-lease arrangements. Restrictions began to ease in 1950, but were finally lifted only in November 1954. The delay was beneficial to the developers. It enabled land to remain cheap, and they sat tight until the repeal in 1954 of taxes on 'betterment', the rise in value of land after development, introduced by Labour in 1947. Commercial land prices doubled overnight.[5] The 1947 Town and Country Planning Act allowed buildings to be rebuilt to their pre-war bulk, plus ten per cent – the so-called 'Spiv's charter', and of which Richard Seifert was the supreme maestro. The LCC allowed 1.7 million square feet of new office space in 1951, but 5.9 million in 1955. Developers did not have to tell landholders of a planning application so they could build up large plots piecemeal in secret. They stretched the credit system, borrowing short term from clearing banks for site acquisition then taking long-term mortgages from insurance companies. In order to avoid paying income tax many of the bigger operators sold 26% of their capital value on the stock market, with their insurance company backers taking a share of the equity. Capital gain on deals was not taxed until 1962, so that there was no tax on re-

Figure 2. Nottingham's Pearl Assurance building, erected on the city's only bomb site, was one of the city's first modern concrete slabs, and was described in the early 1960s as a 'glass palace'

development so long as the new buildings were leased rather than sold on.[6] This was good for the developers, and good for the big insurance companies like Norwich Union, Pearl and the Prudential who provided much of the funding. Behind these massive deals there lurked also a disarming naivety. One of the largest entrepreneurs, Jack Cotton, ran his show with two typists, an accountant, some clerks and a set of files he kept on the spare bed in his room at the Dorchester Hotel.

That there was a need for change there is no doubt. Already in the 1930s local shops were being replaced by the first 'multiples', including Woolworths, which expanded from 81 stores in 1919 to 768 by 1939, Burton's and Timothy White's. And growing numbers of motor vehicles were already causing congestion in many city centres. Visiting central Coventry in 1933, J.B. Priestley found 'ample remains of the cutlery, cloth, button, clock and ribbon periods scattered about, now oddly mixed up with Lyons, cheap tailors, Ronald Colman, cut-price shops, berets and loudspeakers.'[7] How were chain stores and car parks to be squeezed in too? Two new roads were cut through central Coventry to try to relieve the congestion, Corporation Street in 1931 and Trinity Street in 1937, and plans made by Donald Gibson and his wife in the winter of 1939 suggest that the city's medieval core would have been radically remodelled regardless of the war. Bristol saw more disfiguring alterations in the 1930s. Part of the Floating Harbour (the River Frome, controlled by locks since the 1800s) was infilled to make a gyratory traffic system and an area for new office development, and the eighteenth-century Queen Square was bisected by a new road.

The domestic market grew steadily in the Fifties. The economy was sufficiently buoyant to create a new working class in full – if often tedious – employment, with money to spend in their leisure hours. These were the people for whom the new city centres and new housing were aimed. Car ownership doubled between 1947 and 1957, and had increased again by the same amount by 1962.[8] The Sixties opened with an unquestioned belief in new technology, and in progress as a simple and continually upward curve. The mood is expressed in Alan Sillitoe's *Saturday Night and Sunday Morning*, published in 1958 and made into a film by Karel Reisz in 1960. Arthur Seaton, played by Albert Finney in the film, looked favourably at the changes that had occurred in his father's lifetime. Instead of unemployment, there were Woodbines, plentiful beer and paid holidays, even if this hedonism was set amidst the world of the H-bomb and Billy Graham.[9] With the end of conscription in 1961 the prospects for the young seemed even rosier. The set for the filming of

6. Oliver Marriott, *The Property Boom*, London, Hamish Hamilton, 1967, especially p.11. Rodney Gordon's article expresses this point more graphically.

7. J.B. Priestley, *English Journey*, 1933, quoted in Kenneth Richardson, *Twentieth-Century Coventry*, City of Coventry, 1972, p.277.

8. Colin Buchanan et al, *Traffic in Towns*, London, HMSO, 1963, pp.9–19.

9. Alan Sillitoe, *Saturday Night and Sunday Morning*, London, W.H. Allen and Co., 1958, reprinted 1975, Star Books, pp.26–8.

Figure 3. Flats in Nottingham by Drury's of Leicester, 1966, on the set of *Saturday Night and Sunday Morning*

Saturday Night and Sunday Morning was an area of derelict terraced housing in Lenton, Nottingham, which was then replaced with five tall blocks of flats by Drury's of Leicester, completed in 1966.

One town in the south personified this new consumer culture architecturally. Croydon, whose self-proclaimed 'Manhattan skyline' is so redolent of Sixties redevelopment, is a good example of a borough that planned early. 'Croydonisation' was a symbol of civic pride commensurate with the redevelopment of the town's High Street and building of its grand town hall in the 1890s. It began in the 1930s with proposals to build a new road parallel to the High Street on an abandoned Southern Railways freight depot, together with sports facilities and other civic amenities. Robert Atkinson was appointed consultant in 1937, but little was built then save for the gas and electricity showrooms in Wellerley Road, the latter to Atkinson's design. In 1943 a reconstruction committee was appointed and in October the council launched a fifty-year plan which widened Wellesley Road and Park Lane, and Croydon's sunset strip was born. 'We insult our intelligence and fail in our duty to poster-

Figure 4. NLA House, Croydon. Richard Seifert and Partners, 1968–70

ity if we shrink from the obligations that modern conditions impose. This is a bold scheme because the needs of the town demand boldness', claimed the *Croydon Advertiser* in 1945.[10] Croydon's success was in seizing the demand for offices, an opportunity missed by the new towns. In a series of plans for the London conurbation, culminating in the Development Plan for the County of London approved in 1955, the idea gained ground of moving offices and their workforces out of central London. In 1958 the government produced a further report, *Offices on the Move*. To avoid delays in referring compulsory purchases to the Minister of Housing and Local Government, Croydon went for a private Bill in Parliament, which became the Croydon Corporation Act in 1956. The first new building was Raglan Squire's Norfolk House, completed in 1959. In 1964 George Brown on behalf of the new Labour Government stopped further office building. The 'Brown Ban' had little effect on Croydon, where most of the big projects were already under contract and could therefore go ahead; it simply ensured that the offices were leased at premium rates on their completion. In the years 1963–73 20% of offices and 30% of jobs which moved out of central London relocated to Croydon.

To serve the offices further improvements were made to the roads. An underpass was excavated in 1963–4 where Wellesley Road and Park Lane joined George Street, by East Croydon Station; in 1965–9 a flyover was constructed at the southern end of the town centre, and Wellesley Road was widened again. Writing of the underpass the *Croydon Times* commented that 'It felt good. To see the excavation eating huge mouthfuls of earth and rubble and then spewing them into the back of a lorry. This was the march of progress.'[11]

The County Borough of Croydon reaped the benefits of stable local politics. Whether these were Labour or Conservative mattered little. Croydon was Conservative, and redevelopment was led by Sir James Marshall, Leader of the local party from the late 1930s until 1961, and Chairman or Vice-Chairman of most of the committees concerned with the town's development. Sheffield could point to equal continuity from its solid Labour base. But in Birmingham the main parties were evenly balanced. After a long period of Unionist dominance under the Chamberlain family until 1940, Labour and Unionist (Conservatives from 1953) attracted almost equal support. Labour held power from 1952 until the early 1960s with a small majority and the city's redevelopment was the slow, steady result of consensus politics. Both parties sought to build large numbers of houses and to develop a central commercial and retail district while keeping the rates as low as possible.[12] We will see that the strongest evidence of planning policy changing with that of political power is to be found in Newcastle, where the three main parties succeeded each other in turn, and it was evident in Liverpool too.

The prosperity of the Fifties found its way into the local authority coffers of the Midlands and south. This is well seen in the rebuilding of central Coventry, with its high standards of architectural design and public art, although there was additionally government compensation for war damage. Other cities, notably Liverpool and Newcastle, were awarded Development Area status with grants to attract new industries. Everywhere government grants towards capital projects were a far more important factor in the local economy than before the war, particularly for education, health services and the fire brigade. But these were counteracted by the derating of industry by 75% after the war, a government imposition reduced in 1958 and abolished completely only in 1961.[13] This restriction was another encouragement to industrial cities to diversify their economies by attracting compensatory high rates from commercial and retail developments. And domestic rate income was also falling in most cities, with their old-fashioned housing and declining populations.

Birmingham had been noted in the inter-war period for its progressive social programme and swathes of new, low-density housing. It was among the

10. *Croydon Advertiser*, 12 October 1945, quoted in Oliver Harris, *Cranes, Critics and Croydonisation, The Reshaping of Central Croydon*, Croydon Local Studies Library, 1993.

11. *Croydon Times*, 15 November 1963.

12. Anthony Sutcliffe and Roger Smith, *History of Birmingham, vol.III, Birmingham 1939–1970*, Oxford University Press, 1974, pp.57–119.

13. ibid., p.64.

first authorities to include an inner ring road as a key planning policy, for which it began acquiring land in 1943, although it was only in 1956 that it finally began building. The Birmingham Corporation owned large areas of the city centre, but whereas a similar situation in Coventry led to the imposition of a strong formal plan by the City Architect's Department, in Birmingham councillors did not want to discourage developers by laying down a rigid planning scheme. They preferred to offer developers complete freedom to design what they liked, and then to negotiate modifications at a late stage in the planning process. Once a developer's interest was aroused in a site, he would often then agree to extend the area of Corporation freehold land by acquiring adjacent privately-owned sites and passing them over. When building sites were cleared along the ring road, the City became even more concerned to attract new development. However, the first three sites to be marketed prompted only three offers. It was thus fortunate that one of these came from the builders John Laing and Son, working with the local developer Jo Godfrey, who offered to take over all three sites and to prepare a single coherent scheme. The result was the long, ribbon-like six-storey development of Smallbrook Ringway, designed by the local architect James A Roberts. It was among the first examples of a new kind of speculative modernism that was busy, curvaceous and altogether 'pop' in its styling and easy admittance of signage, shop window displays and frequent alteration.

Godfrey, as JLG Investments Ltd, went on to be the developer of the Bull Ring Centre, persuading the Corporation to demolish its nineteenth-century Market Hall and to offer the huge site thus created at a relatively low ground rent. The final scheme developed by Sydney Greenwood and T.J. Hirst in 1961–4 was less elegant than that originally devised by Roberts in 1958, but when it opened in 1964 it was called 'one of the most advanced and successful shopping centres in Britain.'[14] One element that survived from the original scheme, and a condition of the council, was a circular tower at its junction with New Street. The result, first intended to be twelve storeys and heightened by Roberts to 24 after work had begun on the foundations in 1960, was the Rotunda, the most distinctive landmark of the new Birmingham.[15] The result of this very flexible attitude was that far more of the city was rebuilt than in other big provincial cities like Manchester, Liverpool and Leeds, though all faced a similarly constrained city centre and shortage of shops. Birmingham's Architect's Department, under Alwyn Sheppard Fidler, was not consulted about the development; instead the Public Works Department under Herbert Manzoni helped the developer to obtain a maximum of rentable floor space.[16]

14. ibid., pp.443–4.

15. *Architects' Journal*, 4 February 1960, p.188.

16. Sutcliffe and Smith, *op.cit.*, p.448.

Figure 5. Bull Ring Centre, Birmingham. Sydney Greenwood with T.J. Hirst, 1964

A rather more planned development is that of the eastern part of the Calthorpe Estate, the privately-owned enclave west of the city in Edgbaston, where a group of office buildings were developed under the aegis of the estate's architect, John D Madin. 'Birmingham claims, perhaps with good reason, that it has become a city of this century, and that it now contains more buildings of our own time than any other city in Britain, or perhaps Europe.'[17] So wrote a historian as late as 1971, as the last developments – notably Seifert's Alpha Tower begun that year – belatedly joined the skyline, but the ebullient optimism and international comparison are characteristic of the whole Sixties.

A smaller scale of redevelopment can be seen in central Liverpool and Manchester. In Liverpool the main central development was again on land owned by the Corporation, again the central wholesale and retail markets. This time the property company involved was one of the biggest in Britain, Ravenseft Properties Ltd, set up by Louis Freedman and Fred Meynard in the 1940s to develop provincial high streets, beginning in the blitzed cities of Bristol, Exeter and Plymouth where licences were most readily available. Insurance companies provided backing.[18] In Croydon Ravenseft developed the Whitgift Centre on land belonging to the Whitgift Hospital in 1965–70. In Liverpool a deal was agreed with the city council in 1960, with James A. Roberts as architect, and a scheme designed in 1962 began construction in 1966. St John's Precinct, with its 400ft high Beacon bar and restaurant wrapped round the development's boiler flue, was intended to 'place Liverpool ... in the forefront of "modern" cities.' In 1962 Alderman H. Macdonald, Chairman of the city's Development and Planning Committee, commented of the pedestrianised shopping that 'these plans are unique. There is nothing like this anywhere in this country, nothing even in Europe, outside Venice.'[19] The design of the Beacon is based on Rotterdam's Euromast, built in 1960 for an international horticultural show. Graeme Shankland, the city's Planning Consultant, had sent a postcard of it to his planning team in late 1961. But Liverpool's version is taller. St John's occupies a pivotal place in Shankland's master plan for the city centre, published in 1962, and featuring pedestrian walkways and vehicular underpasses. The vertical separation of pedestrians and vehicles is a crucial part of all city centre planning from this time, but because it was conceived so late the Liverpool plan is a curious mixture of new public building funded by speculative projects already approved, and was centred on the creation of an underground rail loop for trains and an inner-city motorway.

Neither Liverpool nor Manchester enjoyed the prosperity of Birmingham in the Fifties and Sixties. Manchester was less badly bombed than the others, and also less comprehensively redeveloped. In part this was a recognition of the solidity and distinctive character of Manchester's Victorian architecture, however unfashionable. Manchester most closely followed London's premise of concentrating new development, particularly high development, at certain points rather than adopting a plan of wholesale rebuilding. Manchester moreover exemplifies the problems faced by northern cities of struggling to modernise while losing their traditional economic base, with the rapid decline of the textile industry in the early 1950s followed by the loss of its docks in the 1960s. In Manchester the decline was never sufficient to prompt the special grants available to Development Areas such as Merseyside and the North East, but it was nevertheless very real in manufacturing. Ian Nairn complained that regional buildings were being designed by London firms with less care than if they were building in the capital, without explaining that higher rents in London allowed for better materials and detailing to be used.[20] In London Alexander Fleming House was unusual in being built at only £5 per square foot, whereas in Manchester this price was normal. Elizabeth House, by the local firm of Cruickshank and Seward (1959–60), is a good example of a prominent building – opposite the Town Hall – that had to be built cheaply and intended

Figure 6. Beacon Restaurant, St John's Shopping Centre, Liverpool. James A. Roberts, 1966

17. Bryan Little, *Birmingham Buildings, the Architectural Story of a Midland City*, Newton Abbot, David and Charles, 1971, p.42.

18. Marriott, *op.cit.*, p.60.

19. *Liverpool Echo*, 20 September 1962. Venice was also used to describe the proposed pedestrian segregation by walkways envisaged by the City of London. Information from Oliver Cox.

20. Nairn, op.cit., p.112; John J. Parkinson-Bailey, *Manchester, an Architectural History*, Manchester University Press, 2000, p.177.

stone panels substituted with coloured laminates.

Formal planning in Manchester concentrated on the creation of a new civic centre with a new public square, the centre being particularly short of open space. This idea had its origins in 1934, with a processional route from the Town Hall to new law courts, but was partially relaxed in favour of a more informal layout in 1962. A new office precinct centred on the Cathedral was then proposed for the western edge of the city bordering Salford, but was realised only haphazardly with the formation of Shambles Square in the 1970s. The one large bombsite, on the west side of Piccadilly Gardens, was filled with a brash development, including a hotel, restaurant, offices, shops and a car park – all the ingredients of Sixties high living – in a 'fuzzily humanistic' melange of heavy board-marked concrete and Sixties plastics, disjointed shapes and constructivist planes.[21] Inside, the King Cotton bar was decorated with murals depicting the local industry, while above it was King Arthur's Court, a suite of three inter-connected rooms and garden terraces intended for dinners and cocktail parties.[22] The joyousness of this kind of Sixties architecture will be appreciated only after Piccadilly Plaza, built in 1963–5 by Covell and Matthews for Bernard Sunley and partly demolished in 2000, is sanitised by an intended recladding scheme.

Where new development followed the existing street pattern, many blocks included a first-floor podium with a linking walkway so that pedestrians could walk in safety above the traffic. Portland Street was to be rebuilt as an underpass. Anticipating this, new offices were built alongside, linked by a walkway, among them a branch of the Bank of England by Fitzroy, Robinson and Partners with a fourteen-storey office tower (1966), and William Deacon's Bank by Harry S. Fairhurst and Partners, with trees on the podium roof (1965). The other local firm building commercial properties was Leach, Rhodes and Walker, who experimented with such new methods of fast construction as continuous poured service cores to save costs.[23] Concrete framing, with lightweight curtain walling, was found in the early 1960s still to be cheaper than steel. Manchester was not spared from having an Arndale Centre, inserted into its central grid in the 1970s, but the Sixties development was piecemeal and incomplete. Above all, the presence of so many headquarters buildings ensured a better standard of commercial architecture for Manchester than for other northern cities. The Ministry of Housing and Local Government established its first regional centre, with the opening of Albert Bridge House in 1962. The largest of the Leach, Rhodes and Walker buildings were dedicated offices for a

21. Nairn, ibid., p.115.

22. *Architect and Building News*, vol.227, no.46, 17 November 1965, p.15.

23. Dennis Sharp et al., *Manchester Buildings*, Manchester Society of Architects, 1966, pp.23–4.

local engineering firm, while the presence of the Co-Operative Insurance Society and Co-Operative Wholesale Society ensured that Manchester got two of Britain's best offices of the Sixties, built in 1959–62 by John Burnet, Tait and Partners.

Money was also a common problem facing the northern cities' housing programmes, but so too was land. The impetus of British planning, embodied in the Garden Suburbs movement, was for a dispersal to the suburbs where large estates of two-storey semis were built with large gardens but few other social facilities. In the 1920s large tracts were incorporated into the cities by means of boundary extensions secured by local Acts of Parliament. In the 1950s these became almost impossible to obtain as government policy sought to limit sprawl by green belt policies. Sheffield is a good example. Its housing problem was one of slum clearance as much as one created by wartime bombing, with up to 35,000 new homes being suggested. But it was acutely short of land. The city boundaries were tightly drawn and the surrounding county councils were reluctant to give up agricultural land to Sheffield's further growth; in 1951 a Bill to extend the boundaries southwards was thrown out on a point of principle. Moreover, the problem had been aggravated by previous housing initiatives, for in the inter-war period and even in the 1940s Sheffield had built a lot of decent, if dull, houses at very low densities. Even in 1966 the percentage of the population living in flats was notably lower than that for the other major English cities. The Park Hill and Hyde Park flats countered a real problem of suburban sprawl. There was, furthermore, a problem that if too many voters migrated to the country, the cities would lose their political power. London was too big to care about this but in the north, especially where there were rivalries between neighbouring cities such as Leeds and Sheffield, to be bigger was to be stronger.

Liverpool had been short of housing in 1939 – 29,000 applicants were on the waiting list – and the situation worsened in the 1950s. Couples were marrying younger and wanted their own homes, and government directives encouraged slum clearance rather than actual additions to the stock. Most important of all was the political message that 'peace must mean progress'.[24] Because of its location it was even harder for Liverpool than for other major cites to expand its boundaries, and like other authorities it found that the building of inter-war cottage estates as at Speke had been greedy with the available land. Liverpool did invest in building outside its boundaries, developing Kirkby under the 1952 Town Development Act,[25] but once that was completed in 1958 the number of new housing units built annually began to drop. Indeed in many places an

24. Ronald Bradbury and Liverpool City Architect's Department, *Liverpool Builds: 1945–65*, Liverpool City Council, 1967.

25. The Government refused to designate Kirkby a new town, and consequently did not provide investment.

Figure 8. High-rise flats in Everton, Liverpool

26. Miles Glendinning and Stephan Muthesius, *Tower Block.*, London, Yale University Press, pp.164–5; *Liverpool Builds, op.cit.,* p.45. Liverpool changed from Labour to Conservative in 1961, which prompted policy changes. Information from Oliver and Jean Cox.

27. Glendinning and Muthesius, ibid., pp.257–8.

28. John Barsby and David O'Brien, 'The Changing Face of Nottingham', in *Nottingham Topic,* vol.3, no.27, p.43.

29. *Architecture East Midlands*, no.6, February/March 1966, pp.6–9.

30. *Nottingham Topic, op.cit.,* p.41.

early 1950s peak of house building was followed by a trough in the late 1950s.

In 1956 the Housing Subsidies Act gave added subsidies for building above two storeys on a sliding scale that increased with height. In March 1954 a deputation from Liverpool visited housing in New York, and subsequently the council built its first tall blocks, Coronation Court and Creswell Mount. By 1963 fifty multi-storey blocks had been built, about 25% of the total accommodation and forming part of a Radburn system of traffic separation as well as an example of mixed development. The council believed too that 'multi-storey blocks offered more scope for industrialisation and the use of tower cranes and hoists' – a belief that if industry was becoming more automated then it was appropriate to use modern factory techniques for housing too. Just as in the 1940s, a mixture of philosophy and actual shortages informed the development of system building – one estimate in 1961 put Britain as having just three days' supply of bricks. In 1962 Liverpool councillors visited Paris and inspected the three most advanced systems of precast concrete construction then in regular use. In 1963 they made a contract with Unit Camus Ltd, who had a license in Britain, for 2,486 dwellings in six 22-storey blocks and 16 blocks each of fifteen storeys, with 1,206 garages. Camus opened a factory near Liverpool to produce these blocks, which were completed in 23 weeks and officially opened in November 1963. Liverpool was the first large northern authority to use prefabricated multi-storey blocks as a way of solving the housing and land shortage, also justified as a means of keeping working-class and sectarian communities in their traditional locations.[26]

Many authorities produced still more mundane solutions. Salford, Manchester and Oldham – arch rivals set side by side and equally opposed to losing their populations, Exchequer Equalisation Grant, rateable value and municipal prestige – experimented with local package-deal towers. Crudens' Skarne system and the 12M Jespersen developed at Laing's Oldham factory – used at St Mary's there and in Manchester's Hulme – were the main systems chosen by local authorities for the wave of deck housing that followed with the imposition of cost yardsticks in the late 1960s. Salford completed 1,468 dwellings in 1966 and maintained a momentum into the 1970s, building the highest per-capita number of new flats of any borough in the country.[27]

Rebuilding was a demonstration of every provincial city's fight for identity in a world of creeping internationalism. It was also a means of hiding the fragility of the sixties economic bubble in an exotic show of concrete high-rises and underpasses. Nottingham, its mentality epitomised by *Saturday Night and Sunday Morning*, demonstrates the fightback of bloody-minded regionalism perfectly. It had three post-war targets – all conceived as early as 1943: a new civic centre north of the shopping area, the merging of its two railway stations as one, and new roads. Projects conceived in 1952 included a sports stadium and helicopter station. In a frantic bid to stop Leicester overtaking it as the major city of the East Midlands, Nottingham gave developers a free hand to build tall offices, and though the lack of a cohesive city plan was widely attacked it could boast that its central rateable value had increased from £4,767,820 in 1961 to £14,642,553 by 1966.[28] A City Architect was appointed only in 1964 and a Chief Planner only in 1966. In 1966 *Architecture East Midlands* called for the building of a system of raised walkways to separate pedestrians and traffic, such as Leeds, Manchester and the City of London were already attempting.[29] That year the *Nottingham Topic* proclaimed that 'not before its time Nottingham has joined the Brave New World Brigade. It has taken on a go-ahead air which has literally transformed parts of the city beyond both imagination and recognition.'[30]

Nottingham's Victoria Centre, filling the vast cutting made for the largest station of the Great Central Railway, fulfills many of Reyner Banham's concepts of the megastructure: mixed use, vast size and adaptability, and it was

Figure 9. Victoria Centre, Nottingham.
Arthur Swift and Partners, 1966–71

five times the size of Birmingham's Bull Ring. It was built in 1966–71 to the designs of Arthur Swift and Partners, a local firm. Early drawings even show part
of it perched over a three-lane motorway project.[31] The Victoria Centre com-
bined a shopping centre and car parking, privately financed by Capital and
Cities Properties with British Railways, and 22-storey blocks of council flats.
The council went on to develop its own Broadmarsh Shopping Centre,
together with Town and City Properties, designed in 1965 by Turner Lansdown
Holt and Partners and opened in 1973. This was still more damaging to historic
Nottingham, as it was built over the best surviving medieval streets. Councillor
Crammond summed up contemporary attitudes: 'Nottingham has to be
altered. We don't like destroying ancient parts, but what can we do with traffic
proliferating at this rate?'[32]

But Nottingham's most radical development was in housing, when under
its new City Architect, David Jenkin, in 1966 it became the fourth city in the
Yorkshire Development Group, founded in 1961 by Leeds, Hull and Sheffield.
Together the cities proposed to built over 4,500 dwellings, one of the biggest
housing contracts in western Europe, and designed to save £750,000 by economies in scale. YDG was unusual in that it was run by the cities' respective City
Architects rather than by housing or education departments, and had its own
team of architects that under Martin Richardson developed a strongly architectural idiom. This owes something to Richardson's own experience working
for the LCC at Morris Walk, and to the model of Sheffield's Park Hill, for YDG
developed a system of medium-rise deck access flats, but using its own precast
building system. In 1967 work began on the first 647 flats of an intended thousand on the edge of Nottingham at Balloon Wood. The scheme offered flats
with either a garden or large balcony to higher standards than the Parker
Morris recommendations, and good internal finishes and fittings. But Balloon
Wood was remote from the city centre, and as early as August 1969 the
Guardian Journal was describing the estate as 'looking like a barracks'.[33]
Rising costs, political changes and the collapse of Ronan Point in May 1968
curtailed the scheme, which was never completed and its social facilities were
never built. The contractors, Shepherds, rashly under-budgeted and construction was poor. By the 1980s the problems of leaks caused by shrinking panels,
condensation, expensive heating and insect infestations were so great that the
flats were demolished.

Most famous of all redevelopment programmes, because so late and so
politically charged, was that of Newcastle upon Tyne. When they succeeded a
Progressive (Liberal) council in June 1958 the new Labour leaders found there

31. ibid., p.58.

32. September 1968, from a cutting held
at Nottingham Local Studies Library.

33. *Nottingham Guardian Journal*, 13
August 1969, from cutting file L33, held at
Nottingham Local Studies Library;
Architects' Journal, vol.152, no.36, 9
September 1970, pp.571–2.

34. Newcastle City Council Minutes, held at Central Library Newcastle, T370, Acc.589, 16 December 1959.

35. ibid. The criticism was lead by the Liberal member, Alderman McKeag.

36. *The Builder*, 21 April 1961.

37. *Industrial Architecture*, May 1963.

38. Cuttings held at Tyne and Wear Record Office, Newcastle.

39. P.W. Macfarlane, 'Capital of the North-East', in *Town and Country Planning*, vol.30, no.8–9, August-September 1962, pp.336–9.

40. The Central Library was designed by the Edinburgh-based practice Spence, Glover and Ferguson; the Herschel (Physics) Building at the University by the London practice (later Sir) Basil Spence and Partners.

was no control of city centre planning, but a free for all. Scotswood Road was being cleared for rebuilding but there was a shortage of other sites and the city had lost a bid to expand its boundaries. A key speech set the scene, delivered in December 1959 by the Chairman of the Housing and Town Planning Committees, one Councillor T. Dan Smith.

> *We live in a city which is a potential goldmine, and it astonishes those of us who are Socialists that you who talk about vested interests and private enterprise have been living on top of a goldmine for ten years and have failed to exploit it. You talk about the cost to the ratepayer. The cost of not developing Percy Street and Northumberland Street is measured in millions of pounds. There is no city of comparable population that has the turnover of Newcastle.*[34]

Smith is accused of 'thinking pink and talking blue' and responds, 'I would rather believe in Clause Four than Charles Clore'.[35] Nevertheless he wanted Newcastle to become what Cliff Michelmore on the BBC's *Tonight* programme in November 1962 called 'the new Brasilia', with new shops and housing.

Parts of central Newcastle are remarkable survivals, with seventeenth-century buildings down by the waterfront and a substantially intact early nineteenth-century retail area (Grainger Town) on the hill above. But the area to the east and north of this had been cut through by roads following the building of the Tyne Bridge in 1925–9, and offered an opportunity for further road building. At the end of 1960 Wilfred Burns, who had been chief planner at Coventry, went to Newcastle to set up a City Planning Department. In early 1961 the first report of the big changes envisaged for the central area appeared.[36] The aim was to 'deal boldly with the City's difficult traffic situation by providing a complete system of urban motorways' with attendant shops and car parking.[37] In April 1961 the Newcastle *Civic News* explained the problem in the context of the times. 'Yuri Gugarin thrilled the world by becoming the first man to go into space and return. He had in fact been round the world in 108 minutes. By contrast the people of Newcastle were *inching* slowly towards factory and office.' The same day there was published what the *Evening Chronicle* described as 'news of a space age Newcastle – the plan for the redevelopment of the city centre.'[38] If men could reach the moon in the Sixties, then what chance had Newcastle of remaining undisturbed? 'Newcastle's structure is largely worn out *as a whole*, and the huge scale of redevelopment needed involves a process of central area revolution rather than evolution, in order to create within relatively few years a fine city centre that will function efficiently for succeeding generations.'[39]

With the roads would come a series of prestige developments by imported architects of international significance at nodal points. This rejection of local individualism is a factor in the visual emaciation of regional cities at this time. The change began at King's College, which in 1964 became Newcastle University, and where Basil Spence was commissioned to design the Physics Building. Between 1957 and 1962 an eight-storey tower and podium, clad in slate, was built on a prominent site that had been the corporation tram depot. Further schemes followed for Spence's London and Edinburgh practices. One scheme of particular local significance was the All Saints Office Precinct, devised in 1969 by Spence and Philip Bennett for Ravenseft, a cluster of indifferent offices (with T.P. Bennett and Partners as executant architects) set round the handsome eighteenth-century church of All Saints. Again prominent because of its rising site rather than particularly tall at ten storeys, only two blocks of the intended redevelopment were completed. Spence was also responsible for the new central library (1968), which replaced that of 1884 demolished for the creation of the urban expressway John Dobson Street.[40] Above the new road the twenty-storey Bewick Court was designed to bring a residential population back to the city centre. More ambitious still was Robert Matthew, Johnson-

Marshall and Partners' Swan House of 1970, its seven floors of offices set over a podium that spanned the expressway on 84-foot steel trusses and which incorporated a crude concrete replica of Dobson's Royal Arcade of 1831–3.[41] The council's coup would have been to have a thirty-storey hotel by Arne Jacobsen in Eldon Square, which he designed in 1967.[42] Fortes were brought in to finance the project, but the firm's merger with Trust Houses caused delays and rising inflation ended the scheme.[43]

Smith also identified that Newcastle was suffering particularly acutely from the exodus of population from the northern cities to the surrounding satellite towns and countryside. 'Take population trends. The Town Plan says the population will be 300,000 in 1972. If we carry on as we have been doing, it will

not be 200,000. It will be in Killingworth.' Killingworth was an unofficial new town built by Northumberland County Council to replace jobs lost in the contracting coalfields. In 1960 the Ministry of Housing and Local Government gave approval to the redevelopment of West Moor and Killingworth under the 1952 Town Development Act, less generous than the 1946 Act in terms of government funding. Most of the area was wasteland reduced by mineral exploitation to what was described as a rural slum. Killingworth is the forgotten English Cumbernauld, a development of housing and a shopping centre based on walkways and pedestrian segregation to create the most comprehensive megastructure in Britain. Reyner Banham makes no mention of it, though he recognises the significance of Cumbernauld town centre, designed by Geoffrey Copcutt in 1960 and built in 1963–8 with shops, civic amenities and flats in a single, deliberately indeterminate mass over a bus station and car park.[44] Killingworth was a still more complete megastructure, a whole town centre and flanking housing conceived as a single unit with walkways over the main roads, developed by fifty architects, engineers and surveyors appointed by Northumberland County Council under the leadership of Ray Gazzard.

There is a strong similarity with the conceptual Hook New Town, a model new town conceived by the LCC that was refused planning permission by Hampshire County Council but which was nevertheless published and enjoyed a wide influence. But Hook was designed to fill a valley, with shops set over an express road; Killingworth was nearly flat, and hence the pedestrians had to clamber across bridges via narrow walkways. Another problem with what was termed 'castle town' Killingworth was not just its massive size and novelty, but the harshness of its precast construction, in many ways similar to that of YDG. 'To complete the township in ten years it will be necessary to build

Figure 10. Swan House, Newcastle, rising above the A1(M). Robert Matthew, Johnson Marshall and Partners, 1968–70

Figure 11. Killingworth Shopping Centre, photographed in 1992 after the adjoining flats had already been demolished

41. *Architect and Building News*, vol.7, no.1, 3 September 1970, p.41.

42. *City News*, September 1969, p.3, in Newcastle City Archives N536(B). I am very grateful to Grace McCombie for extensively researching this for me.

43. Kenneth A. Galley, 'Newcastle upon Tyne', in Holliday, *op.cit.*, p.227.

44. Reyner Banham, *Megastructure*, London, Thames and Hudson, 1976, pp.168–71.

through wet winters and a special system of construction has been designed for the purpose and will be supplemented by various building aids and techniques on site' claimed the *Killingworth Township Handbook* in 1965.[45] To the revisers of the *Buildings of England* it was 'a set for Fritz Lang's *Metropolis*.'[46] Rarely fully tenanted despite long waiting lists elsewhere, after years of gradual abandonment and dereliction, the housing, built by the Crudens (Skarne) system from 1967 onwards was demolished in 1989, the shopping centre in 1992.

'Manhattan', 'Venice', 'Brasilia' or '*Metropolis*'? These are ambitious models for any redevelopment programme, particularly when supported on falling rate income. Much of this development was inspired politically, by government policies on housing grants and by bids to disperse offices from London. High-rise and system-built housing was the product of the 'dash for growth' prompted by extra grants from the Chancellor of the Exchequer, Reginald Maudling, after the slight recession of 1961–2. Keith Joseph, head of the MHLG, had been a director and then Chairman of Bovis Construction in the 1950s, while Geoffrey Rippon at the Ministry of Public Building and Works went on later to be Chairman of Cubitt's Construction Systems in 1964–9. The Conservatives certainly knew the building world, and believed that investment in system building could unlock economic development in town centres as well as providing extensive employment in its own right. The response by Harold Wilson, opening the Science Debate at the Labour Party's Annual Conference at Scarborough early in October 1963, seems comparatively naive in 're-stating our Socialism in terms of the scientific revolution … The Britain that is going to be forged in the white heat of this revolution will be no place for restrictive practices or for outdated methods on either side of industry.'[47] For him building was a smaller element in his vision of a new Britain.

It is thus easy to see the Sixties redevelopment schemes wholly as an expression of greed and expediency. But this was also the 'space age'. In the *Age of Aquarius* and of Apollo it was equally possible to put men on the moon and to envisage a new town as more than a concentration of practical and utilitarian functions. There was a desire to meet psychological needs too, and in the most ambitious developments elements like modern art and design had an important place. This can be seen in Victor Pasmore's work at Peterlee, and in particular at his Apollo Pavilion, conceived in 1963 and opened the week that Apollo 11 set off to land men on the moon. Victor Pasmore believed that in the 1960s Peterlee had no need for a church, but could enjoy 'an architecture and sculpture of purely abstract form through which to walk, in which to linger and on which to play; a free and anonymous monument which, because of its independence, can lift the activity and psychology of an urban housing community on to a universal plane.'[48] The Apollo Pavilion characterises the ultimate 1960s' vision of a conceptual, thought-provoking and better world where it was proposed to provide material necessities and high art for everyone. So far have we understood those ambitions that in the 1990s a local Peterlee councillor asked the Territorial Army, *Jim'll fix It* and *Challenge Anneka* for the Pavilion to be blown up. What were the Sixties trying to achieve? Historians ask 'why did the architecture fail?' They should also ask 'Why did we fail to live up to it?' For while consumer aspirations have continued to evolve, most people are now less, not more, aware of the aspirational qualities embedded in the best architecture of the Sixties. Only in 2002 is there finally a glimmer of hope for what is now known only as the Pasmore Pavilion.

Figure 12. Pasmore Pavilion, Peterlee. Victor Pasmore, 1968–9

45. Northumberland CC, *Killingworth Township Handbook*, 1965.

46. John Grundy, Grace McCombie, Peter Ryder, Humphrey Welfare and Nikolaus Pevsner, *The Buildings of England, Northumberland*, Harmondsworth, Penguin Books, 1992.

47. Quoted in Harold Wilson, *Purpose in Politics*, London, Weidenfeld and Nicolson, 1964, p.27.

48. Victor Pasmore, *Victor Pasmore*, London, Thames and Hudson, 1980, p.230.

7 | Modern Architecture for the Masses: The Owen Luder Partnership 1960–67

RODNEY GORDON

Modern Architecture for the Masses: The Owen Luder Partnership 1960–67

RODNEY GORDON

To establish the background to the cultural climate of the Sixties, one must go back to the post-war period of the late Forties and Fifties, a time very different from today. It is important to understand the social climate that pervaded this elated country at the end of the Second World War. In the dark days of 1941, when the Nazi threat was overwhelming, the whole country had closed ranks and pulled together like one large protective family, a culture which continued into the post-war period. Such an atmosphere is difficult to describe, but to a schoolboy growing up during the great war of good against evil, the feelings of egalitarianism and concern for all was the norm.

The post-war period was an exciting time, a time of great aspirations. The task of rebuilding our blitzed cities was about to be carried out with the energetic spirit of a new society. The old hypocrisies were crumbling, Labour had been swept to power, and a new world was to be reconstructed for the new age, an age of the people.

The thirty years from 1945 to 1975 in my opinion produced the most exciting creative period in the arts this century. I remember my tutor and mentor, the old Bauhaus architect Arthur Korn, clearly articulating in his German accent that 'Architecture throughout history has always expressed the nature of the society in which it was produced.' Looking back at what was built in the Sixties, I realise how true that axiom was. This first age of mass culture, as we at the Architectural Association in the Fifties believed it to be, could not depend upon traditional architectural forms. The country could not afford hand-crafted and expensive materials. Now was the time to give full reign to the ideas of the Twenties and Thirties. The Modern Movement with its base firmly hooked into logic and reason was to me the natural and honest method of building. *L'Ésprit Nouveau* would at last triumph. How gloriously naive we were.

Although I still consider the three great architects of the twentieth century to be Le Corbusier, Frank Lloyd Wright and Mies van der Rohe, only Le Corbusier's work seemed to me to offer the appropriate key to the new architecture. I believed that an architecture that depended upon sculptural concrete was commensurate with the severe economies necessary when building for the masses. For, when everything else is stripped away, the concrete is still needed to hold the building up.

I qualified from the AA in 1957 and was fortunate to get a job in General Division at the London County Council. In those days, the new, exciting architecture was coming from the public sector and for any young aspiring architect, the LCC was the place to be. Housing Division's Killick and Howell were building the Alton Estate at Roehampton; Schools Division had gone Danish-Modern; while General Division was designing the National Film Theatre, and was shutter-board concreting up the South Bank around the Festival Hall.

The first slab blocks at Roehampton had been completed and we were invited to visit the site a few days after the first tenants had moved in. These blocks were superb, the first British manifestation of Corb's philosophy adapted to an English environment, constructed in a rolling parkland setting. I had watched them going up and looked forward to seeing their being lived in. What a shock! The windows were covered with dainty net curtains, the walls were covered with pink cut glass mirrors and 'Kitsch', and the furniture comprised ugly three-piece suites, not even the clean forms of wartime Utility furniture. The new tenants looked uncomfortable. They were in conflict with their surroundings and it was wrong.

I was stunned. From that point, I was forced to realise that these people, possibly quite naturally, had no idea about what the new architecture had to offer and were bewildered by this new environment which were being foisted upon them. The British, unlike our continental cousins, seem to have a desire to live in some kind of romantic mythical past. They prefer fake traditional homes in which to keep their high-tech Hi Fi, television and video. Open any Sunday newspaper supplement today and see the homes on offer, proud of their Edwardian detailing, Georgian porches, and fake half-timbering. So it was on that day in the late Fifties when I realised that architecture for the masses, at least residential architecture, would be only a dream and that people might accept modern architecture to work in, or to be taught in, but not to live in. Being an optimist, I retreated to the view that two points out of three ain't bad and I thanked my lucky stars that I was not working in Housing Division! I remember reading at the time that some American medical statisticians had discovered that the second highest occupational disease amongst professionals was lunacy amongst architects, no doubt brought on by impossible frustration.

It was in 1959, while I was working on my design for the Faraday Memorial at the Elephant & Castle,[1] that I was approached by Dennis Drawbridge from Maintenance and Improvements Division to meet a private-sector developer's architect called Owen Luder. Dennis explained that the E. Alec Colman Development Company had asked Luder to design an entry for the Elephant & Castle Shopping Centre competition. Dennis had been ghosting for Luder doing his working drawings, and Owen was seeking a designer to produce his entry for Colman.

I should say at this point that to us at the LCC the private commercial sector on the whole represented the antithesis of creative architecture. Private sector buildings were either the heavy, bland neo-classicism of the 1930s or, even worse, crude, insulting references to modern Miesian architecture. The

1. A steel transformer station for the London Underground in the middle of the traffic island, so named because Michael Faraday was born nearby.

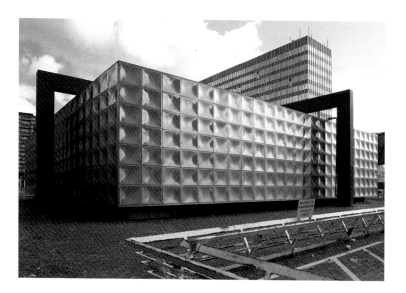

Figure 2. The Michael Faraday Memorial, Elephant & Castle, London, 1959 (Elain Harwood)

neo-classicism of the Thirties was proving too expensive for the speculative developer and certain commercial architectural firms, who shall be nameless, were becoming extremely successful by not designing their buildings. They were bastardising the Miesian philosophy, designing – no, producing – crude, ill-proportioned, naive, matchbox buildings, taking the elevations and whatever else that was pre-designed by manufacturers straight from their catalogues and making good money for the developers and themselves.

At that time, I found it rather strange that unlike other professions, where if you are a brilliant surgeon or barrister you receive wealth, peer group and public acclaim, architects who were producing good architecture like Peter and Alison Smithson were having to make do with just the peer group acclaim. With a certain trepidation I decided to meet Owen Luder and see what the Devil's Kitchen looked like from the inside. The bait of designing a major shopping centre was too strong to resist. Owen was an amiable bloke who spoke developer language in a cockney accent and as I later realised spoke it better than most developers. He appeared to be very good at his job and was obviously poised to obtain a lot of work. Although, as I expected, he did not seem to understand my aesthetic approach (I don't think he ever did), he implied that I had a free hand to produce a scheme provided I fulfilled the brief, which was basically to maximise the amount of shopping and keep the cost to the minimum acceptable level. I can't remember much of the detail of the scheme I produced, but it was the forerunner of the Portsmouth Tricorn Centre and Gateshead. I used the natural multi-level access points to create a three-level shopping scheme and allowed the shoppers to locate themselves in this 'casbah' (Owen first used the term about this scheme) by incorporating a needle-like tower block of offices which could be seen from any point in the complex. Above, I placed a cinema and art gallery that was developed from my student thesis design for a co-ordination centre for architects, engineers and artists at Woburn Abbey, which similarly had had a folded slab roof.

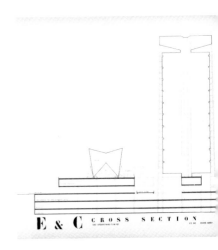

Figure 3. Competition entry, Elephant and Castle Shopping Centre, 1959

With no little apprehension the day came for me to present the scheme to Alec Colman. The drawings were laid out on the boardroom table and as I explained the scheme in detail I was received in complete and ominous silence. The quantity surveyor then gave his costing report, and Owen and Alec Colman picked up their pencils and began to discuss and calculate the feasibility. Then, to my enormous surprise Alec Colman beamed at me and said something like, 'The scheme works a treat financially. I don't want to know about the architecture, but the planners might like it. Get on with it.'

I left the meeting shell-shocked. In a little over one hour a decision had been made to proceed. I had just spent six months sending designs for the Faraday Memorial to committee after committee and still did not have a clear way forward. If the E. Alec Colman Group were anything to go by, architecture could be produced in the private sector. It was the failings of architectural practices working in the sector that was producing the rubbish, not the developers! We did not win the competition.

Alec Colman was a great character whom I later got to know and like quite well as a kind of father figure. I remember one day his taking me aside and saying 'Rodney, if you want to make money, give up architecture and become a developer.' He explained. 'A developer is like a prostitute, you've got it … you sell it … and you've still got it!' I realised at that point that I was never going to be a millionaire.

In the autumn of 1959 Owen asked Dennis Drawbridge and me to join him full time. He would run the practice and bring in the work, I would design it, and Dennis would build it. The Faraday Memorial had finally got the go-ahead and my design work was complete. After three years at the LCC it was a good time to go. However I became ill with jaundice and was confined to bed for ten weeks. I agreed to join him on 1 January 1960. In the meantime he sent me the brief for Eros House, Catford, and I designed this office and shopping scheme from my sick bed.

Eros House was the first and possibly the most important building I designed in the Luder era, as it defined the architecture of all that came later. The site was still covered with the war-damaged remains of the Eros cinema, a massive former theatre, and since demolition was not scheduled until the building contract began, it was not possible to survey the exact site area. The maximum developable area was based upon a 2:1 plot ratio and I considered it part of the brief to give the client the largest developable area possible. In the absence of an initial survey, I conceived the idea of designing an elevation with random cantilevers between the structural bays of two, four and six feet. Thus, by varying these projections after demolition when the exact site area was known, I could provide the client with a building area maximised to the last square inch. The architectural form would come directly from the client's requirement.

I had been informed by the quantity surveyor that speculative office buildings had to have a minimum elevational area for cost reasons. This principle was obviously responsible for the eruption of the crude, mundane, matchbox buildings I so detested. I argued that if I were to express the structure and the services on the exterior in brute concrete, it would not cost more as these elements were necessary wherever they were built. To my pleasure and Luder's surprise his costing analysis proved me right. Little did I realise it at the time, but because I expressed the structure and services externally, my Eros building has since been called the forerunner of High Tech architecture.[2]

At Eros House I realised that the quality of the shutter-board concrete work was likely to be very poor, as the budget for this work fell far below the work we had been doing at the LCC on the South Bank – and even that had not been up to the standards of the Swiss bridge builders like Maillart. I therefore consciously detailed the elements – the exposed beams, columns and floor slabs – to provide a convoluted sculptural form which dominated to such an extent that the quality of the finishes became less obvious. The shops at ground floor level were separated from the offices above by a clear storey of open car-parking, thus expressing the building's different uses. By constructing the vertical circulation in a separate campanile-like tower with bridges linking it back to the offices exploited to the maximum this new-found freedom from the matchbox syndrome.

The last part of the Eros House composition was to build a supermarket for Sainsbury's, their first I believe. Today, it would be considered too small even to be called a minimarket, but at the time it was a great innovation. It sat adjacent to the main complex and being only two storeys high I gave it a shutterboard concrete overhanging roof which curved up to provide the dynamism which it needed to fit next to the much higher office block. We used this detail later on the car-park towers of the Tricorn Centre and Gateshead.

On 1st January 1960 I duly joined Owen Luder, whose office at that time was in a tenement flat in Regency Street off the Vauxhall Bridge Road in London. The office consisted of Owen, myself, Dennis Drawbridge, an office lad and a secretary. Before I had had a chance to complete the general arrangement drawings of Eros, I was inundated with new projects. Owen was brilliant at bringing in the work. To solve the problem of the extra workload, the office was expanded along the lines which in my opinion initially brought great success but also sowed the seeds of its decline. I was made a partner responsible for design and co-ordination, and I developed the Design Section responsible for work up to detailed planning permission. Dennis Drawbridge was made partner responsible for the production of working drawings and site works, and he ran the Working Drawings Section. Owen, as senior partner, would bring in the work, make office policy and oversee the costings of both the work and the office.

At about this time I remember attending a seminar at the AA where I was now teaching. The seminar was given by Ernö Goldfinger, who bemoaned the fact

Figure 4. Eros House, Catford, 1959–62

2. By Elain Harwood in an unpublished report for English Heritage.

3. Being the architect of a listed building has the unfortunate attachment of making one feel like a very old man!

4. A great friend of mine at the time was the film director Mike Hodges and he used the multi-storey car park at Gateshead, while under construction, in his film *Get Carter.*

Figure 5. Turnpoint, Burwood Park,
Surrey, 1961

that Corb-type concrete buildings would never be allowed by the planners in
Britain. Having just received planning permission for Eros, I indulged in a
quiet giggle and thought, 'we shall see'.

We moved to larger offices in Tachbrook Street and as the Design Section
expanded I employed creative people like Peter Abbott and Laurence Howard
as my senior associates. Peter's brother Laurie, Malcolm Wood, Victor Wybrow
and later my present partner Ray Baum, amongst quite a few others, also all
joined. By 1967 the Design Section had a team of about twelve and Owen Luder
had a total staff of sixty.

In 1961 I built a house for my own family in Burwood Park, Surrey, which
was spotlisted in 1997.[3] I have often been asked how I can reconcile its apparent delicate design with the brute concrete buildings I was designing for Luder.
However, if you look carefully it follows the same clear philosophy. It expresses
the structure externally and even mimics the double beams of Eros House. At
my house, the wall finish is the same inside and out, and the whole was designed to be mainly prefabricated and bolted together on site. Building in steel
and timber allows for a much more accurate and delicate result.

Those were happy days. Owen kept the work pouring in and although he
kept a tight control on costs he never interfered with our designs. We worked
flat out, quite often through the night, the next day and the next night to
produce the schemes that bore Owen's name, listening to The Beatles' latest
album to keep us awake. The Beatles were an interesting phenomenon in
themselves. Their albums were enjoyed by six- and sixty-year-olds, by bankers
and bin men. In retrospect, their music was the first true manifestation of an
art form for the masses, the first world-wide art form that everyone enjoyed.

Eros House received the RIBA Bronze Medal for London in 1962. We
designed and built office blocks and shopping centres in Bromley, Hayes,
Hounslow, Hammersmith, Coalville, Leicester and places I can no longer remember. We produced many more projects that never saw the light of day. All
were designed on the basis of the philosophy of Eros House and the Elephant
& Castle Shopping Centre submission, and they culminated with the projects
for the Tricorn Centre in Portsmouth and Treaty Centre in Gateshead.[4]

The Cadbury-Brown architectural practice asked if the principals and some
of the associates could be shown over the Eros building. In showing it to them,
I was surprised and embarrassed to find that the mistakes and errors in the
building screamed out at me, yet my visitors did not seem to be aware of them
and were quite complimentary. You must remember that, if we were to survive
in this competitive sector, our speculative buildings had to be designed and
detailed in the same timespan as those of our competitors. Other speculative

Figure 6. Offices at Hounslow, 1963
(Sam Lambert)

Figure 7. Eagle Star Offices, Sutton, 1967

Figure 8. Offices in Bromley, 1968

5. Ian Nairn, 'Flamboyance in Concrete', in *The Observer*, 1967, undated copy held by Rodney Gordon.

Figures 9, 10. Unbuilt schemes for Luton and Tel Aviv

developers' architects, who produced their buildings from manufacturers' catalogues, spent far less time in the design and detailing stage, so a certain crudeness was implicit in the concept. This taught me the hard lesson that next time we had to be better.

Up until the Tricorn project at Portsmouth, all our designs for shopping centres followed the Developer Rule Book, which listed rules which were never to be broken. The first rule was that a new shopping project had to be built as an extension to an existing successful shopping street. Not even the wrong end of a shopping street was allowed. This wrong end was usually marked by either a railway bridge or the Co-op, or both. For some reason the Co-op always got it wrong! Yet at Portsmouth we were given a site for a major shopping and multi-use scheme that was the shape of a huge rugby ball, bounded on one curved side by Charlotte Street, a very narrow secondary shopping alley containing market stalls, and on the other side by an impenetrable dual-carriageway. Ours was not to reason why. Alec Colman and Owen were the development experts. My job was to design the scheme and not ask questions. Peter Abbott was my number one on this project and we proceeded to design what would now be called an out-of-town shopping centre with car-parking over the top giving direct access to the shopping below. The Tricorn Centre was the last scheme on which I was allowed freely to send members of the design team into the WD Section ensuring continuity into the detailing, and I suppose marked the high point of my work in the Luder Partnership. Unfortunately, the day the Tricorn building contract was completed was also the day that the Partnership began to decay.

Our breaking the first rule of the Developer Rule Book meant that no multiple stores like Marks & Spencer would lease the larger spaces, and the small shops that normally followed their lead were never occupied. This was a tragedy, as the scheme needed the light and shiny shop fronts to contrast with the bold rough concrete forms. Despite recent attempts to resurrect the Tricorn – which I still believe could be done, despite its inclusion in an exhibition of architecture of the Sixties at the Museum of Modern Art in New York, and despite the great support of the Twentieth Century Society and the Portsmouth Society, it is now scheduled for demolition. Was it a fiasco? Ian Nairn certainly thought not, loving the building 'as an animal, various and cranky, capable of inspiring recognition and affection … Owen Luder's team could just go out and *do* it and I personally am glad that the first really successful no-holds barred explosion has come not from one of the in-coteries but from a large firm working to a commercial budget.'[5]

We were finally asked to design a housing project where an enlightened client agreed to consider a housing scheme based upon our architectural approach. The scheme was for about fifty houses somewhere north of London.

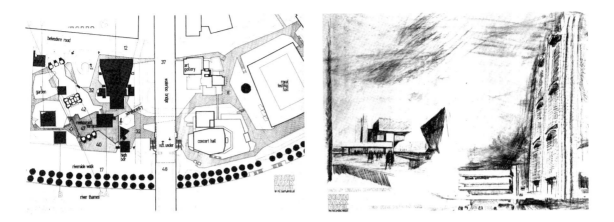

Here at last was my chance. Was I going to be able to solve the architecture-for-the-masses residential problem? The scheme I produced consisted of inter-locking courtyard houses, although the exact details have now faded from my memory. At the meeting when the project was presented, I was pleased to find that it was received by the client with a degree of restrained enthusiasm. Even the agent agreed that the houses were most attractive. Then came the question of selling price. The agent said that quite honestly he was unable to give a price: maybe they would sell for £18,000, maybe for £16,000. Then, pulling some papers from his briefcase, he said 'If you build these neo-Georgian style houses, you will sell them for £17,575, because I have just sold thirty of these for exactly that price!' A developer is in a risky business and must reduce his risk options as much as possible. Need I say which scheme he plumped for?

The office had moved again, to much larger premises in St. George's Square and the Design Section began to become isolated and lose contact with the Working Drawings Section. Owen could not see my point, that design needed to be detailed in sympathy with the concepts, as this was time-consuming and he felt that it affected the office's profitability. My authority ceased once work

Figures 11, 12. Plan and perspective for a conference centre and hotel project, an entry to LCC invited competition for the South Bank (National Theatre site), 1962

Figure 13. Tricorn Centre, Portsmouth, 1966

Figure 14. Treaty Shopping Centre, Gateshead, 1967

progressed to the WD Section. Dennis Drawbridge who ran WD was under pressure to keep the office costs down and the architecture was suffering. When new WD offices were opened in Harrogate and Newcastle under the control of Ron Worthington and Ron Jones to produce the working drawings for Gateshead and other schemes in the north, I was becoming outnumbered. Continuity of the design was all but cut off, and I began to cringe, as did members of my team at what was being built. Distance did not help the situation.

The practice, or should I say Owen Luder, was now receiving considerable acclaim. Owen always insisted that all work should go under his name, as he felt that this was how public relations worked. I know and have always accepted that architecture is more important than the architect, and because of this I had not particularly minded.

Owen was superb at bringing in the work and apart from cost control did not interfere. I and my Design Section were always allowed a free hand to be creative on as many projects as we could handle. This was reward in itself. However, when we heard that Owen had been invited to lecture architectural students at Cambridge and I believe at other schools, who were expecting architectural philosophy but got dissertations on development techniques and economics, I observed a severe decline in office morale. This was the case especially in the Design Section where we were already deeply concerned that our designs were being detailed with total lack of sympathy. I do not wish to go into the unpleasant details, but suffice to say that I resigned my partnership and left the practice in 1967, followed shortly after by my entire design team. Some of them I am pleased to say have gone on to great things with other practices.

In retrospect, I believe that from 1960 to 1967 we were successful in producing an architectural form for the masses – although we never cracked, nor in this country do I believe we ever will, the residential sector.[6]

6. There is a possible exception to this rule: the prefab. Built in their thousands at the end of the war to house the bombed-out homeless, they were well-designed, modern buildings and in general were accepted by the masses. Perhaps they saw them only as temporary accommodation, although a few still survive today. No doubt there is a message in there somewhere, but as yet I can not fathom it.

8 | Brunswick Centre, Bloomsbury: A Good Bit of City?

PATRICK HODGKINSON

Brunswick Centre, Bloomsbury: A Good Bit of City?

PATRICK HODGKINSON

The design and construction of Brunswick Centre in London spanned from 1959–70 for myself, although building ceased in 1972 with the Centre incomplete. I am pleased that Rodney Gordon has written warmly of E. Alec Colman as his major client, for without this same developer – a man of foresight and nerve – the Centre would never have got off the ground. It is only a sadness that McAlpine's, with whom Colman chose to share this development, should have ousted him as chairman of the development company in 1970 when they also dispensed with my own services equally abruptly. Here, though, I will outline the reasons behind an unlikely dream whose reality, due to those events, became seriously marred.[1] Let me start with art, history and architecture in general.

Figure 1. The Loggia, Brunswick Centre, from Coram's Fields, 1972

1. I lectured informally without notes. Although the Society kindly lent me a recording of the lecture, I have taken the liberty of turning spoken word into prose.

I like to use a painting by de Jong of Old London Bridge, which hangs at Kenwood House in London, as an analogy for town-making. The bridge crosses from the past to the future, its arches providing stability and continuity, both necessary to society at large. Thus far it is permanent, unchanging. Balanced on top, the little houses, like houses of cards that might blow away, represent the transient, 'lifestyle' side of individual needs: the fashionable. Making towns must include both aspects, but today most architecture is just about style and fashion. I do not think this will make well-loved towns, because they will lack continuity.

Here is a painting of a stag, painted around 5,000 BC at Catal Hüyük in what is now Turkey, animals being revered but not considered gods. The same people built shrines with a formality about them, while their clusters of houses were entirely informal. They knew about mood and had distinct souls. While civilisation has brought change to lifestyle, nonetheless art throughout history demonstrates how little we have moved from our ancient forebears in matters of the senses. We are frightened and elated similarly and – who knows? – probably laugh at equivalent things. The 'Bull-Leapers' fresco at Knossos has immediate physio-erotic appeal. Against all that, the idea of hi-tech mankind put about by media spin-doctors is just material-worship.

And so too, from the mid-1950s onwards, was 'system-building', an appar-

Figure 2. Old London Bridge, de Jong

Figure 3. Reconstruction of stag's head in a shrine at Catal Huyuk, Turkey

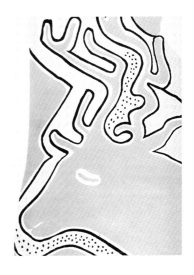

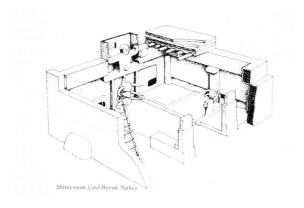

Shrine room, Çatal Hüyük, Turkey

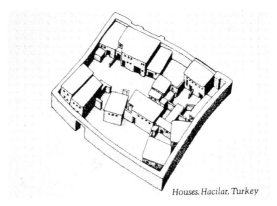

Houses, Hacilar, Turkey

Figure 4. Reconstruction of shrine room, Catal Huyuk, Turkey

Figure 5. Reconstruction of houses, Halicar, Turkey

ently fast and cheap method of constructing through mechanised techniques, where forms and faces of housing and offices, for example, were often indistinguishable. System-building made deserts of urban areas, doing more damage even than had the Luftwaffe. Championed by politicians seeking quantity rather than quality, how grotesque was all this, for since the early eighteenth-century British town-making had been the greatest architectural gift we had given to the world, from Bath to Bloomsbury, Brighton to Belgravia, and Edinburgh's majestic New Town.

Good architecture is good town-making, simply that. And yet, so many post-war planners and architects searching for the new appeared to forget much of that record of sense.

The area of Bloomsbury in which the old Foundling Hospital Estate was positioned comprised badly war-scarred late Georgian architecture, which by the 1960s had become mostly a slum. Before 'conservation' had entered the lingo, our firm was asked to design a replacement for the Estate with far more housing and commerce than former pattern-book development had achieved. But there was a different aspect of that town-making which we rejected, one that tends to be forgotten by those who clamour for preservation at all costs, namely the rigid class system that operated behind those outwardly beautiful fanlights and sash windows where everyone knew their place, most especially women. We felt that late twentieth-century society with its emerging freedoms would need something different, although the ideal of long terraces overlooking open space might well be continued. How then should we cut through the outworn shibboleths to find an expression for today's soul?

Figure 6. 'Bull-leapers' fresco, Knossos, Crete

Figure 7. System-built housing, London,
c.1962

Figure 8. Aerial view of Bath

As a student, I had visited Le Corbusier's Unité d'Habitation at Marseilles in 1951, just before the building was finished. Although I was stunned by the master's poetic realisation for sublime urban life, I did not believe his dream could be a reality for London. He was only interested in *tabula rasa* land – had he not proposed demolishing most of central Paris to make way for his glass skyscrapers? – whereas London needed new housing forms that would blend with its existing stock and street patterns.

Yet *provocateur* Le Corbusier affected minds in different ways. On the one hand, young architects at the London County Council were designing 'mini-Unités' for estates at Roehampton, Brixton and Hackney: eleven-storey slab blocks that aped Le Corbusier's idea but lost his wonderful spirit, jettisoning as well our own good traditions. On the other hand, I, as a student, designed an alternative for the Brixton site using four-storey terraces. They related in scale to their surroundings and yet achieved the same high density as the LCC's high-rise proposal. I had demonstrated that high-rise was not necessary for high density, as was generally thought. In my subsequent research, I found that terraced building, as used by the Georgians, was highly economical of land. Sir Leslie Martin, who had championed the LCC blocks as

Figure 9. Le Corbusier's Unité
d'Habitation, Marseilles, photo 1952

Figure 10. Housing project for Brixton,
Patrick Hodgkinson, 1953

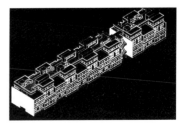

the Council's Chief Architect and who had now opened his own office, therefore invited me to develop my student scheme for a large site in St Pancras. Although this design was not built, it was published.[2] Colman, who had bought the Bloomsbury site but had had a planning application rejected for exceeding the 80 ft height limit, saw the publication and asked us to act for him. As soon as our outline consent was in the bag, I was appointed sole architect for Brunswick Centre to work out the details in London.

The idea of a superblock (megastructure, if you like) had been in my mind since, as a student, I had read Lewis Mumford's notion of building over several New York blocks to exclude through traffic and define a community.[3] In the

Figure 11. Harvey Court, Caius College, Cambridge, Martin Studio 1961

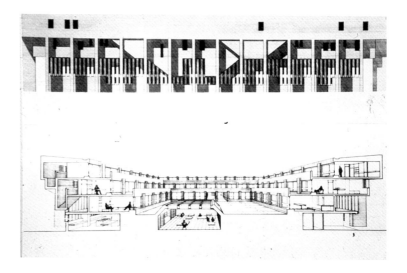

eighteenth century the Adam Brothers had put houses over commerce at the Adelphi. But the most compelling example I knew was the Palais Royale in Paris, with its apartments and chambers over shops surrounding its charming gravelled garden. I also found an engraving of George Merryweather's plan, never built, for the Foundling Hospital Estate projecting two very long terraces, with public gardens between them, from Queen Square in the south to the northern boundary of the estate at, roughly, Tavistock Place. All these affected my thought but I did not draw directly from any one example. The Martin Studio had already designed Harvey Court for Caius College at Cambridge – another idea developed from a student notion – which used a stepped section as its spatial basis. This basis was seminal, but the main aim was to come up with a contemporary interpretation of the terraced eighteenth- or nineteenth-century ideal.

What did the Brunswick design achieve in town-making terms? It broke from the customary habit of zoning housing away from shops and workplaces – a killer of life. It met the highest permitted residential density over a high commercial input, with underground servicing and garages, within the 80 ft height limit. It increased the number of residents from the existing overcrowded, slum conditions, giving back some 75 per cent of the initial site area as public or private open space where, apart from trafficked streets, there was little. With its east-west orientation, the housing's raked section and sloping glass ensured sun in all homes over the middle of each day. Finally, here was the comprehensive plan the planning authority was seeking, stretching from Bernard Street to Tavistock Place, about two-thirds of a mile.

In a world which now considers architecture as art, these functional factors will seem boring. They were not boring to us. The country as a whole still had

2. *Architectural Design*, vol.29, no.7, July 1959.

3. Lewis Mumford, *The Culture of Cities*, New York, Harcourt Brace, 1938.

much substandard housing and traffic was ruining cities. The design of buildings had to show positive gains of real social amenity if architecture was to lead the field. Architecture is town-making, but it is also really just a craft, if we chaps do not rise above our station. Art comes in to affect deeper emotions – matters for the psyche – but I will come to that later.

Colman and McAlpine's sought an entirely speculative development with a large range of leasable housing and a smart shopping street to go with it, including pubs, restaurants and a recital hall whose name would recall that G.F. Handel had lived on the site. As we designed it, the housing in the taller blocks comprised quite lavish penthouses over family dwellings of several different sizes, while the lower, outwards-facing perimeter blocks were to be hostels for student medics and nurses working in the nearby hospitals. This would have produced a rich mixture of people all using the promenading decks, typical of a traditional London village. At the centre of the pedestrian shopping street was what should have been London's first glass-roofed shopping hall as a meeting place for the neighbourhood – as large as the converted Covent Garden pair which came a dozen years later – the roof of the shops becoming not decks but a large area of raised ground with trees and planting for general public use. This would be overlooked by professional chambers, medical surgeries and a crèche approached from the main housing access ways, thus keeping those areas policed by constant use. Under the open loggia facing Coram's Fields the planned recital hall was replaced by a cinema with bars and lavish foyers.

What is this loggia? It is not an entrance, for it leads to nowhere particular, yet it gives shoppers a view of ancient trees and people playing tennis in the sun, a feeling of fresh air. It is a monument with its seven tall pillars. John Ruskin was born in a house on this spot overlooking those trees, but he was not afterwards a frequenter of Bloomsbury. Yet many of those thinkers and writers who gave us the freedoms we enjoy today were connected with Bloomsbury, and from early on in the design process it seemed to me that they should be openly remembered at Brunswick Centre. To commemorate eminent people with statues seemed old-hat. A space opening on to nature seemed more to the point. So the seven tall pillars have meaning.

At the same time we planned a new pedestrian route connecting the Euston Road rail termini to Queen Square and the rising office developments of Holborn, with Brunswick Centre in the middle. We also had London Transport standing by to bring a new exit lift from Russell Square underground station (the platforms run under the shopping street) right into the Centre. All this meant that the developers' letting agents had an encouraging list of retailers wanting to rent space. Even Hatchard's Bookshop wanted an outlet there.

Figure 12. Cross-section, Brunswick Centre, 1972

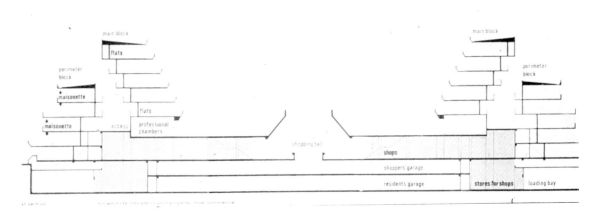

We had secured detailed consensus and were preparing construction drawings when the first blow struck in 1965, the year the new London boroughs were formed.

Whereas Colman saw the point, McAlpine's themselves had never liked the comprehensiveness of the outline consent, preferring something much looser which could involve system-building and change, once uses proved themselves as building proceeded. This was precisely what the LCC was against. The Macalpini did not appreciate the considerable development advantage of making an entirely new place in this central but outworn part of the West End. They now refused to risk putting so much new housing on one site at once. It was a poor decision for, had they gone ahead as Colman wanted, come the boom of the Eighties they would have reaped colossal profits. No. Although much of the site had been cleared and foundations laid, they decided to scrap everything.

With Colman's blessing, I negotiated with Camden Council, whose Labour majority was not too keen about this enclave of Tory development in their midst, to lease all the housing with related garages for council tenant use. The sad bit was that Camden reduced our 15 different housing types to three, making a ghetto, but that is party politics for you. The benefit was that, with redesigned housing to a far tighter budget, a lease was signed the following year whereby Camden advanced the full cost of constructing the housing and its garaging in advance. McAlpine's retained the commercial parts, but now they did not need to borrow money to build the housing. The upshot for the new shopping street, however, was that since the Centre would just be a council ghetto, with all that that meant at the time, the good quality tenants pulled out, including even the original cinema tenant, and a lower-grade Centre became the order of the day.

Despite the disadvantages, I remained enthusiastic because I felt that the future might still bring something better. And it has. In 1965 no-one foresaw that within twenty years council tenants would be able to buy their own leases, selling on to outsiders if they wished. It was unfortunate that in redesigning the

Figure 13. Sectional Perspective, Brunswick Centre, drawn by Peter Myers in 1972

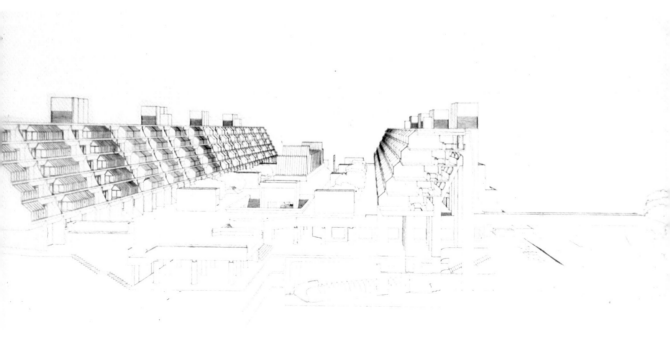

housing to lower costs we lost the special winter gardens. These permitted dual use of frontages as either open balconies or extensions of living space, an idea I had stolen from Brighton, which seemed the perfect answer to our climate. Instead, Camden insisted on fixed balconies.

The important point was that de Jong's Old London Bridge analogy remained. The heavy parts of the structure that were providing continuity went unchanged, but within that matrix we were able to make substantial changes to the housing to suit different lifestyles. To all of us at drawing boards that was a distinct advantage of the initial concept. And that same concept turned out to be man enough not to be rubbished by the further changes which were to come. It happened like this.

In 1970, when construction was well under way, Colman was suddenly removed as Chairman of the development company. The following day I was called into McAlpine's head office. McAlpine's Chairman asked me, 'How long do you need to complete all construction information?' 'One month' I replied, because that was its due date. 'Very well', he said. 'You have achieved all consents, having negotiated Camden's lease. We are contractors and, while we need to be told what to build, we don't need to be told how to build it. Your contract supervision will cease from today, and the day after you hand over the remaining information your commission will be terminated.' I had known of course that, where McAlpine's had a development interest in a building contract, they had done the same to other architects before me: the Dorchester Hotel in the 1930s, for instance. There was no argument nor reprisal I could make as long as my fees to date were honoured.

Not long after I left the job I realised the McAlpine purpose. With Colman and myself out of the way, and with encouragement from Camden's Town Clerk, cuts to the fabric would be made to lower building costs, irrespective of the very detailed final planning consent. The entire complex was being built of the cheapest concrete, which could not stand 'fair face'. It was to have been painted a cream colour, like Regent's Park and the painted dressings of Georgian Bloomsbury. Against that London uniform, the shopping street would have had colour, coloured tiles making a strong paving pattern and facing the circular columns to the arcade, and mosaic and coloured paint to give warmth and glitter at night.

All this was dropped, along with many architectural details important to the concept. The glazed shopping hall, the fountains and the decent entrance to the cinema went too. Finally, all building ceased at Handel Street, with its

Figure 14. Model of winter garden for Brunswick Centre, 1972

Figure 15. Axonometric of council family flat, Brunswick Centre, 1972

unfortunate, sawn-off end. By most of these omissions, McAlpine's shot themselves in the foot, because reputable traders did not wish to trade in such a poorly finished place. To make everything worse, almost no maintenance has taken place in the last 25 years since building ceased.

Despite all this, the initial concept has lived on, and the Brunswick Centre has become loved by many of its residents. While I was the named architect, the concept would not have been realised without the help in my office of a small family of friends, notably David Levitt and David Bernstein, who went on successfully to start their own joint practice in 1970, and Anthony Richardson, who did likewise on his own. I owe them gratitude not just for their hard labours, but for their thoughtful contributions to the concept of the Centre.

An elderly tenant who has lived in the Centre for many years, Roman Malynowsky, wrote to me several times about what might happen next, but we never met until recently. I was standing by the Renoir Cinema, gazing up at the shafts of the loggia, when an old man came out of a door towards me, smiling: 'Are you admiring *my* building?' he asked. 'Well, yes,' I replied, and taking a risk I added 'I'm also admiring *my* building, Mr Malynowsky.' No architect could have wished for more. 'Ownership' of a home we love is natural.

In the early 1990s McAlpine's sold their freehold to another developer who, using different architects each time but never myself, made three attempts to achieve a planning consent to improve and extend the Centre. In principle I am all for this, provided that, as the Bloomsbury Conservation Advisory Committee has said, the new work is 'governed by the initial concept.'

[Editor's note: a fourth scheme, by Hodgkinson himself, led to the building being listed in 2000. Subsequently this was revised by Levitt Bernstein, with Hodgkinson's approval, and received permission late in 2001. The new scheme extends a supermarket across the northern end of the shopping precinct, and constructs a new 'eyecatcher' and entrance to the Renoir cinema by the loggia.[4]]

I will conclude with a word about art which, I believe, should no longer be applied to architecture but should come from within. One of the more perceptive written descriptions of Brunswick Centre came from David Hamilton Eddy and I'll quote from it now:

> Someone like Alfred Teal, who has lived in the Brunswick Centre since 1972 … saw it as a fabulous place right from the start … The magic is to do with escape from the quotidian grind into a poetic and paradisal world, but this is the paradise not of the Garden but of the cerulean blue, the paradise of air, of the free spirit … The Brunswick Centre is transitional … Conceived in the middle of the century it connects the past with the future (that bridge?), in its very structure metaphorical of the movement from one chamber of history to the next. In this sense it is a striking marker of one of those rare true shifts in human sensibility.[5]

'A Good Bit of City' was the *Architectural Review*'s title for its feature on the Centre as building ceased,[6] but I'd prefer to accept Roman Malynowsky's heartfelt opinion.

4. Information kindly supplied by Kevin Murphy at English Heritage.

5. David Hamilton Eddy, 'Castle Mythology in British Housing' in *RIBA Journal*, vol.96, no.12, December 1989.

6. *Architectural Review*, vol.152, no.908, October 1972.

9 | Modernism, Medicine & Movement in 1960s Britain

JONATHAN HUGHES

HEALTH AND HOSPITALS

A SPECIAL ISSUE

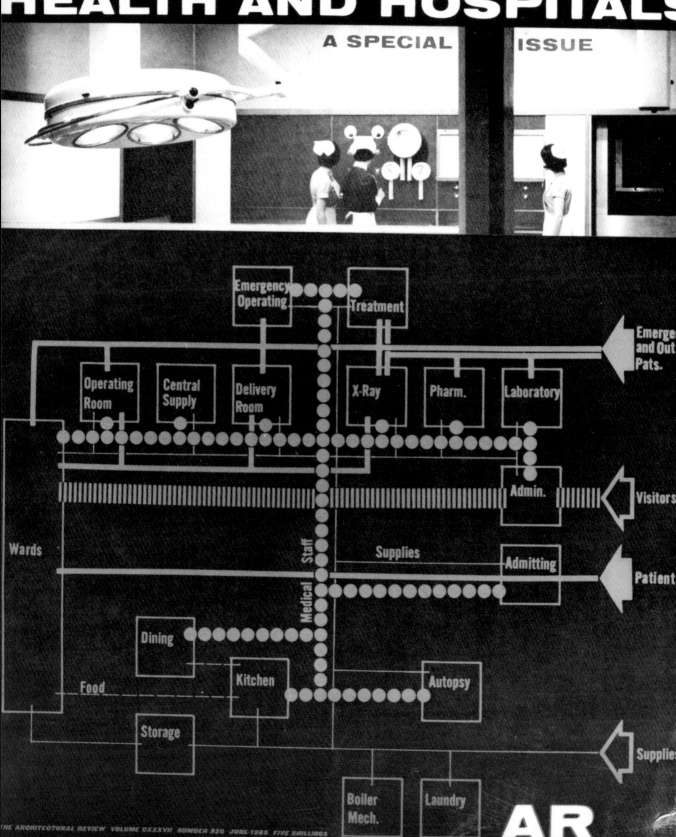

AR

Modernism, Medicine & Movement in 1960s Britain

JONATHAN HUGHES

This article seeks to reconsider the relationship between clinical and civic design as it manifested itself in Britain in the 1960s, and to investigate the similarities and points of contact between what are often considered by their practitioners to be two quite distinct discourses. It aims to do so partly through a consideration of a major representative project: Greenwich District Hospital (1962–74) in south-east London. Most notably, a consideration of the project's zoning of functions and circulatory logic also reveals a profound affinity with the concerns of modernist urbanism.

In June 1965 an *Architectural Review* issue on hospital design featured the ideas of the American pundit of modern hospital planning, Gordon Friesen, outlining ways in which planning and mechanisation might be marshalled to create more efficient hospital buildings.[1] Friesen had been known to British readers from at least 1961 and had consistently argued that various hospital functions could be removed from clinical areas, centralised, and rendered more efficient. For example, the numerous kitchens, traditionally located on each ward, could be replaced by a single whole-hospital kitchen with meals delivered to patient areas by a dumb waiter.

It is not difficult to perceive Adam Smith's invisible hand at work: the systematic pursuance of increased productivity through specialisation and mechanisation, separating off tasks to be undertaken by a dedicated staff whose work might be more easily regulated and controlled. The architectural outcome is clear: the hospital becomes atomised into a series of servicing and serviced departments linked by a network of distribution systems designed to ensure the rapid and efficient circulation of goods about the building. Movement and efficiency are privileged as fundamental concerns of the modern hospital plan.

Within the clinical areas of the hospital, sophisticated techniques of separation and categorisation have also been developed to minimise the risk of cross infection and maximise control, categorising patients by clinical specialty and degree of dependency. Isolation wards have long sought to control disease through physical separation and containment whilst the recent adoption of intensive care units has centralised post-operative care in a single department, as opposed to providing it individually on the general wards. Yet there is a lingering undercurrent of miserable inadequacy to the modern hospital's obsessive pre-occupation with order and efficiency – itself an institution ever devoted to fending off illness, disease and bodily malfunctioning, its chore never-ending.

Parallels may be drawn between medical architecture and modernist urbanism: after all, some hospitals are the size of small towns. As Siegfried Giedion put it in 1951:

> The question of the best size and form a hospital should adopt, in order to give psychic help to the sick and at the same time meet all medical requirements, is somewhat akin to the question of how large a city should be, in order to meet the needs of its inhabitants and fulfil its functional requirements.[2]

Figure 1. Cover of *Architectural Review*, June 1965, showing Gordon Friesen's circulatory logic for the modern hospital

1. See *Architectural Review* vol.31, no.820, June 1965, and also Gordon Friesen, 'Mechanization and Hospital Design', *Architectural Design*, vol.31, no.1, January 1961, pp.7–9.

2. Siegfried Giedion, *A Decade of New Architecture*, Zurich, Girsberger, 1951, p.183.

Most famously, Le Corbusier's 1924 text *Urbanisme* had made explicit the conjunction of notions of circulation, sanitation and efficiency: separating out traffic into pedestrian-free networks of transportation. In addition, the proposed construction of high-rise blocks in open parkland provided an apparently meritorious solution to over-crowded, insanitary nineteenth-century accommodation. Such processes of separation, specialisation and sanitation appear to have become almost indissolubly bound up with notions of efficiency and health, and were frequently rehearsed in British pro-modernist texts of the 1930s and 1940s. Sanitation should be understood broadly as modern society's anæsthetising pre-occupation with safety – and by extension health – witnessed vividly in relation to motor transport, with pedestrians increasingly shepherded behind railings and into subways in order to facilitate the processes of specialisation and geographical separation. Sanitation and health may be proffered in justification but, once more, the not so invisible hand of capital may be sensed, re-organising the spatial logic of the city to facilitate circulation and, ultimately, production.

Conceived and largely built during the 1960s, Greenwich District Hospital was underwritten by notions of throughput and efficiency, and stands as testimony to Friesen's ideas, but there are also valid reasons for suspecting a direct interchange of ideas between British hospital and urban planning of the time. Hospital design did not simply plunder urban models for its own uses; urban theory may itself have owed a debt to medical planning, with both discourses ultimately involved in processes of separation, specialisation and sanitisation indicative of capitalism's need to order and render controllable the phenomena of everyday life.

On a roughly square seven-and-a-half acre site in south-east London, Greenwich District Hospital was most notable for its reticence, being surprisingly sympathetic in scale to the surrounding Victorian terraced housing. Its compactness belied the accommodation inside, including full out-patient facilities and 800 in-patient beds. The external façades were unified by the repetitive module of the structural system, whilst the window wall was recessed some three feet behind this façade. The concrete aggregate finishes of the building's prefabricated structure were enlivened by the display of the stubs on which the internal beams rested but were hardly brutal; whilst between floors, horizontal bands of louvre panels countered the verticality of the structural columns.

Figure 2. Greenwich District Hospital, general view

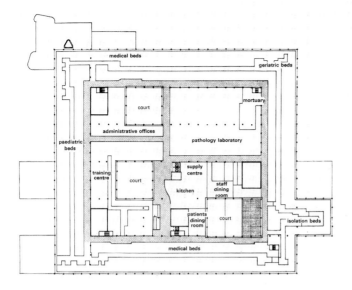

Figure 3. Greenwich District Hospital, typical floor plan. From W.A.H. Holroyd, *Hospital Traffic and Supply Problems* (London, 1968), p.111

Internally, the impression was one of horizontality and spaciousness. However, the main corridors displayed a bland, largely windowless monotony, often apparently left-over spaces tucked in between clinical departments. Such drabness was only countered by the three internal courtyards which the corridor system skirted, offering a welcome distraction, a glimpse of natural light and a means of orientation. The in-patient wards themselves were located around the perimeter of the building, conveying a more reassuring, therapeutic environment, their relatively low ceilings diminishing their institutional feel.

The building was well received, although this was not wholly surprising given that it had replaced the old Greenwich & Deptford Union Workhouse. Extended during the 1930s and bomb-damaged during the War, it was this ramshackle and partially unsound hospital which the Ministry of Health inherited in 1948 under the 1946 National Health Service Act, and whilst it was evident that major repairs were required, funding was unavailable. However, in 1960, the Ministry of Health was searching for an urban hospital site on which to undertake an experimental redevelopment project and Greenwich presented the ideal test-bed. With Ministry and Board co-operation formalised by 1962, plans for the £6m hospital were ready by May 1964 and received positive press coverage.

The project was to fulfil several goals, most notably providing the Ministry's fledgling Architect's Department with its first attempt at whole hospital design (this over a decade after the inception of the NHS). The aim was to rationalise dispersed services on to one site, creating an 800-bed facility approximating to the multi-disciplinary District General Hospital (DGH) envisaged in Enoch Powell's 1962 *Hospital Plan for England & Wales* which had proposed the modernisation of the nation's hospital infrastructure.[3] The project also offered the opportunity to investigate and evaluate Ministry design recommendations, ranging across dimensionally co-ordinated modular systems of furniture and fittings, to the development of a structural system known as the 'Universal Hospital Space'. The latter sought to accommodate virtually any hospital function, from wards to laboratories to operating theatres alike, whilst also being capable of flexible internal sub-division and servicing, offering the ability to change with clinical need. To fulfil these requirements a wide-span beam with an integral intermediate services sub-floor was developed, thereby largely

3. Ministry of Health: National Health Service, *A Hospital Plan for England & Wales*, London, HMSO, 1962.

obviating the need for vertical service ducts which might constrain the planning of the clinical floors.

The Greenwich project was the third to be undertaken by the Ministry of Health following the establishment of its Chief Architect's Department in 1959. It was not until the end of the 1950s, concomitant with the Conservative Party's 1959 election pledge of increased hospital building, that the Ministry formally established its Architect's Department – until then the State had concentrated its resources on house- and school-building. Upon his appointment as Chief Architect in 1959 William Tatton Brown (1910–97) created a series of development teams, reassessing and developing hospital design guidance. Like the Ministry of Education before it, the Ministry of Health published standard design guidelines via its *Hospital Building Notes* (HBNS) and specialised *Health Technical Memoranda* (HTMS). The later HBNS focused on individual clinical departments, offering design criteria ranging from the preferred planning relationships of rooms to minimum environmental standards. These HBNS segregated departments into specialised entities, classifying the functions proper to each and separating off functions which could profitably be centralised. By contrast, the first three volumes published in 1961 took a wider view of the preparation of a hospital's building programme and a description of the services offered by the 600–800 bed DGH, which was to be the basic hospital unit.[4] Clearly indebted to Friesen's schematisation of the hospital this third HBN included flow diagrams linking the individual hospital departments with lines indicative of various traffic flows including patients, staff, visitors, food and supplies (Fig.4).[5] No overall form was suggested for the hospital, but the emphasis on communication and circulation for the efficient functioning of the hospital was clear.

Tatton Brown was well placed to effect Enoch Powell's *Hospital Plan*, having organised reconstruction groups in Burma after the War, and headed Hertfordshire's pioneering schools building programme. Educated at the Architectural Association and a member of Britain's Modern Architectural Research Group (MARS), Tatton Brown belonged to that celebrated côterie of architects so inspired by the 1927 publication in translation of Le Corbusier's *Vers Une Architecture*. Upon completion of his studies, Tatton Brown worked briefly in Paris for André Lurçat – a founding member of CIAM. Lurçat was known for his commitment to the idea of architecture as an agent of social change, a stance shared with his friend Berthold Lubetkin with whom Tatton Brown worked as Chief Design Assistant from 1934–38. After a brief partnership with ex-Tecton member Lionel Brett in 1938–40, Tatton Brown subsequently spent a year with Finsbury Borough Council.

Finsbury was the undeclared location of Aileen and William Tatton Brown's two studies of urban redevelopment published in the *Architectural Review* in September 1941 and January 1942.[6] The scheme proposed the linear reconstruction of an inner-city area, with a string of housing and office towers over a pedestrian deck of shopping and leisure facilities – themselves architecturally integrated with the expressways beneath. Compared to the Corbusian *tabula rasa* approach, the project sought to a certain extent to respect the existing urban fabric by dovetailing the new with the old, creating at their junction an urbanism somewhat characteristic of the collaging æsthetic of the *Review*'s contemporary promotion of the Picturesque.

The Finsbury project's significance lay in the stress it placed on issues later of importance not just to urban planners, but also hospital designers. Most notable was the attention given to the demands of all forms of traffic and the circulatory systems needed to service them. The emphasis on the separation of pedestrians from vehicles was explicit, creating specialised – and more efficient because speedier-routes for cars alone. Also significant was the separation of through traffic from local traffic, creating a hierarchy of major roads

4. 'The Work of the Research & Development Groups, IV: The Ministry of Health', *Official Architecture & Planning*, vol.26, no.2, February 1963, pp.145–146.

5. Ministry of Health, *The District General Hospital (Hospital Building Note 3)*, London, HMSO, 1961.

6. William & Aileen Tatton Brown, 'Three-Dimensional Town Planning', *Architectural Review*, vol.90, no.537, September 1941, pp.81–88, and vol.91, no.541, January 1942, pp.17–20. Also correspondence with the author, January 1995.

serving distributor roads, and the rigorous elaboration of a multi-level architecture integrating the vertically-segregated transportation systems.

Tatton Brown spent the latter part of the War as a Royal Engineer during the recapture of Burma, and subsequently establishing reconstruction planning organisations. The Ministry of Town and Country Planning provided Tatton Brown with his first post-war work as an Assistant Regional Planning Officer (1946–8) under William Holford, forming contacts with Hugh Casson and Colin Buchanan. This was to be cut short by the vacancy in 1948 of the post of Deputy County Architect at Hertfordshire under C.H. Aslin. However, in 1959 Tatton Brown returned to Whitehall to take up a post at the Ministry of Health, where he initiated the hospital building programme.

To furnish architects with design guidance for the hospital building programme the Ministry of Health undertook a series of development projects through which to formulate and test HBN recommendations. Whilst Greenwich marked the first attempt at *whole* hospital design, the Ministry had already undertaken two smaller schemes to assess structural solutions and design guidance – at Liverpool's Walton Hospital (1959–67)[7] and Kingston Hospital, Surrey (1961–7).[8] Both projects employed long-span structural systems to create wide-open internal spaces amenable to flexible sub-division as required. In both cases, the horizontal structural system was deep enough to deliver utilities and engineering services from above or below as required.

Greenwich was the Ministry's third and most ambitious project. With a design team headed by Ministry of Health architect Howard Goodman (1928–99), a process of atomisation, separation, evaluation and definition was applied to every hospital function in the pursuit of the most economic use of labour, time and space in the running of the hospital. The designers' ultimate goal of efficiency was to be met through the structural flexibility of the Universal Hospital Structure and the standardisation of fittings. The freedom required of the Universal Hospital Structure was to be achieved via 64' prefabricated beams incorporating an integral six-foot deep intermediate services sub-floor (on Vierendeel beams). In this way, the clinical floor could be cleared of engineering ducts, thereby permitting the delivery of services to any part of the floor from above or below as desired. The major engineering service risers were rationalised into four vertical service ducts, whilst communications facilities were centralised in a further single 'supply core' (housing the automated goods distribution system, lifts and escalators).

Greenwich's design also evidenced a profound interest in rationalised servicing and circulation systems. Gordon Friesen's automated conveyors, centralised service departments, trolley distribution of goods and other such methods promised the managerial and financial benefits of control, productivity and economies of scale, and were to underwrite Greenwich. As an example, a reduction in the provision of departmental storage space was attempted through the automation of the delivery of supplies from the central stores. Goods entered the hospital at the basement, to be transferred to the bulk stores via a programmable conveyor system. An automated paternoster then distributed goods to individual 'supply centres' on each floor, using photo-electric sensors to 'read' destination cards placed on the containers. The dimensions of the standard container were methodically investigated, its size having to accommodate the majority of hospital supplies *and* be of 'a convenient woman-sized lifting load' (found to be 25lbs, suggesting a container of two cubic feet).[9] The design assumed that only part-time female labour would be available for such work. The architecture of the hospital was therefore partly dictated by and reinforced assumptions about the types of work women would, or could, undertake. The system ceased to function many years ago.

Human circulation about the building was facilitated by three bed lifts, two goods lifts, and a bank of six escalators. The main public floors were planned

7. Ministry of Health job architect Michael Bench, in association with Liverpool RHB architect T. Noel Mitchell.

8. Ministry of Health job architect John Ward, in association with South West Metropolitan RHB architect Richard Mellor.

9. 'Problems and Solutions – Greenwich-II', *British Hospital Journal & Social Science Review*, vol.79, no.4128, 30 May 1969, p.1029.

as a double cubic figure-of-eight (dubbed the 'hot cross bun' principle) converging on the central communications hub where the lifts, escalators, disposal rooms and paternoster 'supply centres' were located. The main corridor route passed by rather than through clinical departments, and as such formed the counterpart of the Tatton Browns' network of routes for through traffic in their *Architectural Review* articles. To complete the analogy, a secondary of system of corridors ran within the departments, notably around the perimeter of the building through the wards. Supply and disposal traffic was not to use this 'local' corridor – supplies being distributed to ward utility rooms whose doors opened on to both sets of corridors. Similarly, waste disposal was

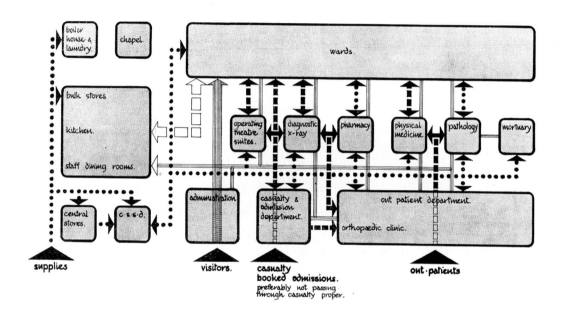

Figure 4. Flow diagram of the District General Hospital, from Ministry of Health, *Hospital Building Note 3* (London, 1961), p.12

effected through hatches for collection by dedicated portering staff outside the department. Whilst beneficially separating clean and dirty traffic, sanitising even further the clinical areas, the plan also acted to segregate grades of staff, thereby specialising and limiting the scope of their employment in true Taylorist fashion.

The wards were arranged as a linear strip around the perimeter of the building, thereby permitting the flexible allocation of beds between clinical specialties, since individual wards could simply be defined as segments of the strip. Such flexibility was dependent on the linear plan of the wards and is surely reminiscent of the recurrent modern architectural interest in the linear city as a means of uniting the multifarious demands of urban design with efficiency of circulation, a lineage which might be traced through Le Corbusier's Algiers Project or the Tatton Browns' war-time *Architectural Review* schemes. Moreover, this preoccupation with linearity was to underwrite numerous British town plans of the 1960s, including Cumbernauld, Hook and Runcorn.

Indeed, the care taken at Greenwich to specialise, separate and render circulation more efficient was paralleled by changes in Britain's urban infrastructure. William Tatton Brown's own wartime reconstruction plans were underwritten by similar assumptions about the desirability of separating people from traffic, increasing the efficiency of circulation, and the ameliorating,

sanitising potential of modern architecture on the environment. Motor transport raised different problems for the State. Post-war governments realised
that rising car ownership would necessitate investment in the road network
and in 1946 the Minister of Transport, Albert Barnes, proposed a ten-year,
£800m programme of motorway building. Effective vehicular circulation
appeared fundamental both to economic health and the redistributive goals of
the Labour government, as well as potentially unifying the regions. The plans
were all but abandoned with the worsening of the economy during the late
1940s, although the 1949 Special Roads Act empowered the creation of roads for
the exclusive use of traffic. Banning pedestrians, these new traffic-only motorways were justified through appeal to arguments of safety, efficiency and the
need for segregation.

Britain's motorway programme was not resumed until the late-1950s. The
Preston By-pass in Lancashire (later part of the M6) was the first motorway
standard road to be opened in December 1958 whilst the first 72 miles of the M1
were opened in November 1959. Indeed, the 1960s witnessed the increasing
specialisation of Britain's roads. In 1960, the establishment of London's Road
Traffic Management Unit introduced major one-way systems, box junctions
and urban clearways to further regulate the users of London's roads, whilst the
1963 report of the Worboys Committee on all-purpose roads added to the
momentum, urging a network of primary routes across Britain.[10] Yet it was
another official publication which was to have the greatest influence on architects. The impact of *Traffic in Towns*, published in 1963, was immediate and
enduring, the volume selling a remarkable 17,000 copies in four months and
being reissued as an abridged Penguin paperback.[11] More importantly, the
publication made explicit a connection between modern hospital and city
planning.

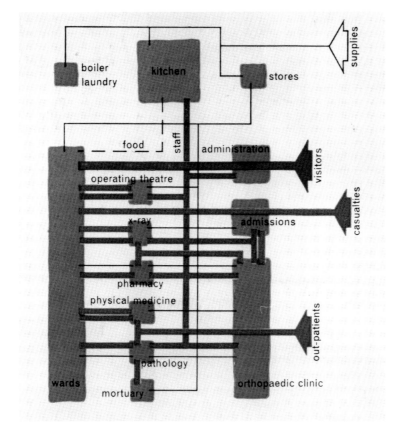

Figure 5. The 'basic principle' from
Traffic in Towns (London, 1963), p.41

10. Ministry of Transport: Traffic Signs
Committee, *Report of the Traffic Signs
Committee*, London, HMSO, 1963,
paragraph 13.

11. Ministry of Transport, *Traffic in
Towns: A Study of the Long-Term
Problems of Traffic in Urban Areas*,
London, HMSO, 1963.

Known as the Buchanan Report, after the chair of the Working Group, *Traffic in Towns* was the final report of the committee appointed in 1961 to consider the problems of increasing car ownership.[12] Coming fresh on the heels of the abortive London County Council Hook New Town project, the report was flush with the optimism of 1960s town-planning, offering daring solutions elaborated in a series of case studies whilst warning that the complete accommodation of the car would be both physically and financially impossible. The report aimed to separate traffic, especially through traffic, from 'environmental areas' such as shopping centres, residential and industrial estates. It combined this with the idea of creating a network of roads equating with the public's 'desire lines' (its unconstrained, preferred routes) – rather than arbitrarily imposing ring and radial road schemes, which had been a typical post-war approach applied at Coventry. Notably, Buchanan's 'traffic architecture' and his emphasis on the separation of through traffic were redolent of the Tatton Browns' *Architectural Review* articles, and whilst it would be incorrect to view *Traffic in Towns* as a reworking of the Tatton Browns' texts (many of the ideas were in wide circulation anyway) it is possible that Buchanan knew of them through the *Review*, or through contact with Tatton Brown at the Ministry of Town & Country Planning.

Most importantly, the analogy Buchanan used to elaborate his strategy was that of the hospital. Using a flow diagram of a District General Hospital from the 1961 *Hospital Building Note 3* (although not acknowledged as such) Buchanan elaborated his 'basic principle'[13] of through routes and environmental areas in terms of the corridors serving hospital department (See Fig.5, cf Fig.4 rotated and inverted). As he put it, food trolleys would not pass through operating theatres on their way to the wards, just as through traffic should not pass through environmental areas. The comparison was a significant one; as hospital designer John Weeks noted in 1966:

> *Analogies with city planning which can be drawn from hospital design are close. The separation of main communication routes from the [clinical] departments they serve is similar in principle to the avoidance of environmental areas' by main roads – one of the principles proposed in the Buchanan Report.[14]*

Buchanan's notion of 'traffic architecture' was accompanied by Kenneth Browne's sketches of schemes for pedestrian decks of shopping and leisure facilities spanning redesigned road systems, at once integrating whilst also

Figure 6. Comprehensive redevelopment scheme illustrated by Kenneth Browne, from *Traffic in Towns* (London, 1963), p.143

12. For a discussion of Buchanan's career, see Michael Bruton, 'Colin Buchanan, 1907–', in *Pioneers of British Planning*, ed. G.E. Cherry, London, Architectural Press, 1981, pp.203–23.

13. Ministry of Transport, *Traffic in Towns, op.cit.*, p.41.

14. John Weeks, 'Indeterminate Hospital Design on Urban Sites', *Hospital Management Planning & Equipment*, vol.29, no.360, June 1966, pp.338–41.

segregating all the circulatory components to increase their efficiency and offer a safer, more amenable environment to the pedestrian.

Buchanan's ideas found their realisation towards the end of the 1960s in the new town at Runcorn in Cheshire (designated 1964). Runcorn's master-plan, by ex-MARS member Arthur Ling, exemplified the logic of separated circulatory systems and functional zoning espoused by Buchanan and CIAM before him.[15] At its heart, the model was once more that of the linear city, with a strip of housing and industrial facilities strung along a communications system now knotted into a closed figure-of-eight. An urban motorway known as the 'Expressway' carried general traffic whilst a separate 'Busway' (a buses-only road network) offered a more local, public mode of transport. Runcorn's housing

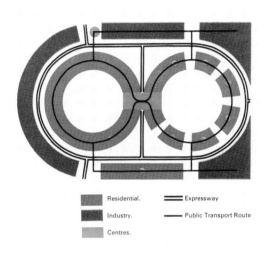

was grouped into separate estates (Buchanan's environmental areas) along the Busway and bounded by the Expressway, the latter separating off the rigidly zoned industrial estates. At the centre of this network was Shopping City, the supply centre of the town, a multi-level communications interchange, shopping and leisure centre, with superstores, a market, pubs and a cinema.[16]

What is striking about Runcorn is not just the whole-hearted adoption of Buchanan's boldest ideas, but the conceptual similarity with Greenwich District Hospital. Both were planned as figure-of-eight circulation systems, converging at a distribution hub, providing shopping at Runcorn and hospital supplies at Greenwich. Both relied on binary systems of hierarchical transportation routes, with two types of road at Runcorn serving through and local traffic and two corridor systems at Greenwich enforcing a similar split. Indeed, just as the wards at Greenwich were positioned around the perimeter of the building in a circuit along the 'local traffic' corridor, so too were the housing estates at Runcorn sited along the 'Busway'; and just as banding at Greenwich utilised the 'through traffic' service corridor architecturally to divorce ward areas from support departments, so too were the housing estates at Runcorn physically separated from the zoned industrial areas by the 'Expressway'.[17] In both schemes specialised circulatory systems served to link segregated functional entities, whilst at the same time acting to separate them. Runcorn's Shopping City embodied the multi-level traffic architecture foreseen by Buchanan, with cars, delivery traffic, buses and pedestrians all arriving on different levels into this megastructural centre, united by lifts and banks of escalators with the main pedestrian shopping floor. In a similar manner Greenwich enforced the separation of patient/visitor and goods traffic by using different mechanical systems to transport them through the building.

Figure 7. Runcorn New Town, Arthur Ling's concept for the master plan, from Runcorn Development Corporation, *Runcorn New Town Master Plan* (Runcorn, 1967), p.20

Figure 8. Shopping City, Runcorn New Town, Runcorn Development Corporation, opened 1972. Vehicular traffic enters at ground level, pedestrians have their own walkways and buses have third, elevated, access system

15. Arthur Ling, *Runcorn New Town: Master Plan*, Runcorn Development Corporation, 1967.

16. Designed by Runcorn Development Corporation (Roger Harrison) c.1967–72. See 'Runcorn Main Shopping Centre', *Architects' Journal*, vol.155, no.25, 21 June 1972, pp.1377–92.

17. Ling's theory did not rule out the possibility of interspersing discrete residential and industrial areas along the local traffic spine; nonetheless at Runcorn these areas were rigidly segregated on either side of the 'expressway'.

Both hospital and town were modelled according to the same principles of sanitised zoning, circulation and efficiency, even making recourse to an identical physical format and implying a common relationship with the body.

There is a final and most telling link between hospital and town-planning of the period. For both parties alike, clear, modern signing systems promised to foster more rapid and efficient circulation. Indeed, the late 1950s witnessed an outburst of interest in signing, from the aesthetic possibilities presented by signs to the new signing systems regulating and speeding movement through the environment. Herbert Spencer, designer and editor of *Typographica*, characteristically bemoaned the 'jumbled jungle of words' on British roads in a 1961 photo-essay of London's signing, demanding graphical discipline, restraint and a cleansing of this visual disorder to sanitise the urban environment.[18]

The necessary clarity was soon to be imposed and, remarkably, it was the work of just one practice which during the 1960s redesigned the signing of virtually every national transport system: Kinneir Calvert Associates, originally formed in 1956 by Jock Kinneir (1917–94) and later joined by Margaret Calvert (1936–). Notably, an early commission was for the signing of Britain's first road, rail and air interchange at Yorke, Rosenberg and Mardall's Gatwick Airport, soon to be followed by numerous airport commissions including the 'rational' house-style for British European Airways and later for the British Airports Authority. Similar signing work was also undertaken for British Railways (including Sealink ferries), with Kinneir again modifying a standard Helvetica typeface into his 'Transport' face.

Kinneir's most prominent work was for the national road networks. Britain's road-signing system dated from 1933 and in 1957 the Ministry of Transport appointed the Anderson Committee to recommend new signing for the first motorway-standard road, the 1958 Preston By-pass. The Committee appointed Kinneir as its consultant and his signs subsequently formed the basis for all of Britain's motorway signage. The Committee's requirement for legibility at both speed and distance were again met by utilising Kinneir's mix of upper- and lower-case sans serif Helvetica-based lettering, a strategy later adopted by Kinneir for his signing work for Britain's all-purpose roads, undertaken for the 1961 Worboys Committee. And so, within a decade, Kinneir and Calvert's signs were directing traffic around virtually every transportation system in the country – not to mention numerous others.

Against this background Tatton Brown launched a Ministry project to prepare a standardised signing system for the NHS. The piecemeal redevelopment of existing hospital complexes had at worst generated labyrinthine routes through buildings, and it was considered that clear signing would help reduce apprehension in a large, unfamiliar building. Unsurprisingly, Tatton Brown appointed Kinneir and Calvert as his designers. Trialed in 1965 at the new Out-Patient Building of St. Stephen's Hospital in London, Kinneir and Calvert's signs sought to combine, as Margaret Calvert has recalled, '*value for money*, clarity, simplicity of application, as well as aesthetic considerations'.[19] The resulting signing system consisted of a series of sign 'planks' capable of flexible combination with a standardised taxonomy of authorised departmental names, symbols and directional arrows – the planks' coloured backgrounds varying with function: brown for general signs, red for Accident and Emergency, and blue for safety. Clarity of definition and standardisation were central to the system; as Kinneir and Calvert's signing manual for the British Airport Authority characteristically stated, 'Communications depend on standardisation. Deviations from the norm give rise to misunderstanding … no deviation [from the system] is necessary or permissible'.[20]

Employing another variant on Helvetica, Kinneir's 'Health Alphabet' typeface was a clear, sans serif face with all the simplicity and anonymity of international Modernism, by now thoroughly shed of any earlier avant-garde

18. Herbert Spencer, 'Mile-a-minute Typography?', *Typographica*, 4, December 1961, pp.3–16.

19. Correspondence from Margaret Calvert, February 1994.

20. 'Introduction', in British Airports Authority, *British Airports Authority Sign Manual*, London, BAA, 1972, n.p.

Figure 9. Health Alphabet, Jock Kinneir, *c.*1965, reproduced in DHSS, Health Technical Memorandum 65 (London, 1984), p.35

connotations. Likewise the sans serif arrow, stripped down to its essentials and possibly derived from Paul Klee's *Pedagogic Sketchbook*, stood as a symbol of the technological age. Indeed, this purity and directness (surely archetypal high modernist concerns) possibly concealed a less distinguished pedigree – sans serif faces having once connoted an even primitive vulgarity. An engraving of a garden setting in Humphrey Repton's *Designs for the Pavilion at Brighton* reserved serif letter forms for the denotation of those things proper to the realm of art, intellect and beauty, whilst sans serif lettering was assigned to the province of the crude, 'natural'[21] world. Surely it is wholly appropriate that the sanitised, clean-cut, efficiency of modernist sans serif lettering might be little more than the flipside of a vulgar, 'natural' baseness, especially in a setting such as a hospital where all the calm, ordered efficiency of functionalist architectural rhetoric is ever compromised by the presence of unpredictable, degenerate, dysfunctional disease. Indeed, this conflict between diversity and singularity, between freedom and control, summoned-up by the very programme of a national signing system, is surely equally indicative of the issues at stake in the programme which underwrote the design of Greenwich Hospital itself, where the ordered clarity of the figure-of-eight corridor system co-existed with the potential indeterminacy of the plan facilitated by the Universal Hospital Space.

Greenwich Hospital has been run down, its facilities transferred elsewhere. Yet for a brief period, between the austerity of the early post-war years and the economic and social retrenchment of post-oil-crisis Britain, a conjunction of relative prosperity and a belief in a scientifically developed modern architecture found its realisation in buildings such as Greenwich Hospital. A logic of separation and specialisation underwrote the project, aiming to achieve efficiency of medical care. The increasing desire to control and cure illness reinforced the need to separate and specialise, to categorise and compartmentalise. Such processes may be viewed as sanitising – minimising the risk of contamination from disorder, and rendering the environment neat,

21. James Mosley, 'The Nymph and the Grot: The Revival of the Sanserif Letter', *Typographica*, 12, December 1965, pp.2–19.

Figure 10. Detail of engraved frontispiece from Humphrey Repton, *Designs for the Pavilion at Brighton* (1808)

comprehensible, and controllable. The techniques employed in the process may be seen to underwrite much broader debates relating to urbanism and town planning, drawing on discourses of efficiency, circulation and sanitisation in their attempts to render our cities more efficient and pleasant. This is not the place to chastise what might now be seen as naïvely optimistic endeavours. Rather, it is to point to the dangers of regulation and segregation implicit in such manoeuvres, seeking to create an architecture of separation, sanitisation and control which can never fully hope to contain all the processes of everyday life and death. Even if medical knowledge and modernist architecture can constantly evolve, so also do viruses and disease. Illness remains as prevalent as ever, ever testing both the medical profession's curative skills and the modern hospital's ability to adapt in response. Modern architecture has sought to cope with such problems, to offer understanding and solutions whilst constantly threatened with change. But the apparent futility of such a constant heroic struggle suggests an alternative view, proposing modernist hospital architecture as one of denial, obsessively seeking to defeat the challenges thrown at it through the valiant declamation of its own efficiency and ability to cope, all vouchsafed by its supposedly scientific validity.

ACKNOWLEDGEMENTS

I should like in particular to acknowledge the assistance of the late William Tatton Brown and staff at Greenwich District Hospital, Kingston Hospital and Walton Hospital in the production of this article. Thanks are also due to Professor Christopher Green at the Courtauld Institute of Art under whose supervision the research for the article was undertaken.

    A longer version of this paper was awarded the Essay Medal of the Society of Architectural Historians in 1996 and has been printed in *Architectural History*, volume 40 (1997): permission to reproduce part of the original paper is gratefully acknowledged.

PHOTOGRAPHIC CREDITS

Illustrations 4, 5, 6 & 9 are Crown copyright, and are reproduced with the permission of the Controller of Her Majesty's Stationery Office. Illustration 3 is reproduced by permission of the King's Fund. Illustration 7 is reproduced by kind permission of the Commission for the New Towns. Illustration 1 is reproduced by permission of the *Architectural Review*.

10 | The Counter–Modernist Sublime: the Campus of the University of Essex

JULES LUBBOCK

The Counter–Modernist Sublime: the Campus of the University of Essex

JULES LUBBOCK

In 1991, having launched the first Prince of Wales Summer School in Civic Architecture, I returned to the University of Essex where I had been teaching since 1971, and underwent my own personal conversion on the road to Damascus. I saw that many of the things we had been trying to do with the Prince of Wales on the Summer School were embodied in an architectural complex which seems at first sight the antithesis of our New Urbanist ideals: the 1960s campus of the University of Essex. I will try to explain what appears to be a paradox.

In the summer of 1992 a group of graduate art history students under my direction produced a report called *A University Renewed.* This made suggestions about how the Essex campus, strongly disliked by a majority of its academic community, could be improved at a minimum of cost. We recommended washing the concrete rather than painting it, clearing litter, improving the street furniture, creating more bars and restaurants. One result: a fine, glazed corridor, facing south over one of the main squares, was recently transformed into an extremely successful restaurant. While they eat, people can now observe the activity in the square below. This project at Essex was based upon one run by Leon Krier, Christopher Alexander, Alan Baxter and myself at Bagnaia, near Viterbo, with the students on that first Summer School in 1991. Since then several undergraduate art history students have produced BA dissertations on the university, and in 1995 we interviewed the first Vice Chancellor, Sir Albert Sloman, the only man who could provide a record of the process of design since the death of the architect, Kenneth Capon.

First, I'm going to give an account, based upon the Sloman interview, of the genesis of the design. Second, I will describe the key features of the master plan and indicate how they related to the architectural issues of the early Sixties. Then I will take you on a very brief tour of the campus, and explain what I mean by the Counter-Modernist Sublime. Finally I want to introduce one or two thoughts about the nature of what I would like to call the Counter-Modernism of the 1960s and its relationship to recent developments. That will help to explain the paradox of how it was that someone could move from the New Urbanist ideas associated with the Prince of Wales, Leon Krier, Christopher Alexander and others back to Essex, and find many of them manifest in our supposedly modernist campus.

The creative process of designing the master plan for the campus was very fast. It was produced in three months, between 1 October and 28 December 1962. It was the work of one man, Kenneth Capon of the Architects' Co-Partnership, and the client was one man, Albert Sloman. There *was* nobody else. They were the only two employees of the university at that time. Indeed, the Academic Plan itself had been produced in a very brief nine months, between December 1961 and September 1962, and in only three months of intensive work. That was the sole work of Albert Sloman.

Essex was one of seven new universities, part of the major expansion of the late Fifties and early Sixties. It was the last to publish its master plan. In 1959,

Figure 1. University of Essex, Square 4, detail from north west. (Steve Cole, National Monuments Record, English Heritage)

Figure 2. Detail of concrete

Essex County Council had proposed their county as one of the sites for a new university. In 1960, a Promotion Committee was formed, met the University Grants Committee, and proposed, as the site for the campus, Hylands Park just outside Chelmsford, the county town. A year later, however, in 1961, Chelmsford was rejected on the grounds that, being close to London, it was feared that everybody would commute. Colchester in the north eastern corner of the county was chosen instead.

Things started moving rapidly in December 1961. The site at Wivenhoe Park, between Colchester and Wivenhoe, was announced; Sir Leslie Martin produced a list of architects for the Promotion Committee; and Albert Sloman was amongst those invited to apply for the post of Vice Chancellor. Six months later, in June 1962, Sloman was appointed. Although he didn't take up the appointment until September he had two immediate jobs. The first was to finalise the details of the Academic Plan because, second, it was necessary to choose and to brief architects. He says that he never *formally* briefed Capon. There was no briefing document. The Academic Plan is explained in Sloman's Reith lectures for the BBC which were written in August 1963, delivered in November and published a year later as *A University in the Making*. It remains an extraordinary document, prescient of developments that have taken place recently in the university sector.

There were four key concepts in Sloman's plan. First of all, the university would be a place of international quality research which would provide the context for teaching. That meant that the university had to be very large because in the sciences large research projects required large departments. So, for a new university starting small, it was necessary to have a few carefully chosen large departments each with a minimum of 20 to 30 staff. Hence the emphasis on bigness: 5,000 students in ten years, 10,000 in twenty years, and even 20,000 was envisaged after thirty years. In fact, in 1996 after 32 years there were only 5,500 students. This has been a major problem for the reasons Sloman anticipated. Second, the university would focus upon modernity, upon what had happened to the world since the eighteenth century, and upon new subjects. Hence the study of the modern world, the comparative study of literature in different countries, focusing upon areas that were not treated at Oxbridge or the civic universities, such as Latin America, the United States, the USSR, the study of sociology and government, computing and applied math-

Figure 3. Model of Essex Campus, by ACP. From A. Sloman, *A University in the Making*, BBC, 1964

ematics. Third, in spite of all this modernity and novelty the university would adopt traditional academic departments and subject disciplines. It wouldn't go for the approach of other New Universities of merging departments into Schools of Study. It would retain academic subjects on the grounds both of social cohesion and academic discipline. But the Schools of Study to which the departments belonged would permit cross-fertilisation both in degree schemes and scholarly research. This system would also allow these subjects, as they developed, to grow together, perhaps to form new departments, or simply to be physically contiguous with one another. It was a favourite theme of the period, the notion of flux – one didn't know what was going to happen. So you had to anticipate, you had to allow for change.

In relation to that, Essex also had a system of what were called Common First Years; that is, in contrast to the pre-existing system where students progressed from O' Levels to A' Levels and then specialised in a single subject at university, when they got to the University of Essex they would have a year which broadened their education. Premature specialization remains a major issue in British secondary and higher education.

Because of these concerns, it was necessary to create the physical basis for a single academic community: a campus which was close-knit. Finally, there would be student flats rather than halls of residence or colleges. Rather oddly there would be no Student Union and no Senior Common Room: everybody, staff and students, would mix together.

Figure 4. Towers with teaching blocks sunk in the valley

Sloman had no *physical* architectural concept in mind, other than a prejudice, having taught there, against the United States campus university with departmental pavilions set in a park, such as you find at Berkeley or indeed at the University of Sussex designed by Basil Spence. Sloman raised the spectre of irritable, rain-drenched dons scurrying from one building to another between lectures. This, he said, was not a pleasant sight and it didn't have pleasant consequences. He was very interested and excited by recent developments in architecture. He had been a Professor and Dean at Liverpool University, a longstanding member of the Development Committee and a close friend of Myles Wright, Professor of Civic Design there.

In late September 1962 interviews were held for the architect and planner of the university. Ten firms were interviewed. Sloman was working to Martin's list, but he had studied and discussed the work of the different firms with Myles Wright. These included the Architects' Co-Partnership (ACP); Howell Killick Partridge and Amis; Powell and Moya; Richard Sheppard, Robson and Partners; Casson and Conder; and David Roberts. Sloman much admired Powell and Moya, but they simply said, 'Sorry, we're too busy.' ACP was the runner-up. The key factor in choosing ACP was that, whereas other leading candidates had prepared outline plans, Capon, when asked what the university would look like, replied, 'I have not yet had an opportunity of talking to the Vice Chancellor. I have no idea what his academic plans are. Therefore, I have no idea what the university will look like.' Sloman liked that very much! Here was an architect who would listen to him.

This was a very hierarchical and perhaps a rather an autocratic way of setting up an institution, but it was very fast. The Promotion Committee, headed by Noel Annan, selected Sloman. Sloman worked out the Academic Plan. Sloman, with the Committee, selected the architect. The architect designed the physical plan to fit the Academic Plan. There were no other staff, before the founding professors and the Librarian were appointed in April 1963. They all fitted into the Academic Plan. They then selected staff for their department, and the students came along and got what Sloman and Capon had designed. It has more or less continued on Sloman's lines and, despite teething problems, Essex is a success, academic and social.

So the master plan was a *fait accompli*. It is often claimed that Capon

Figure 5. The Library, seen from the south with Wivenhoe Park behind. (Steve Cole, National Monuments Record, English Heritage)

simply followed the outline of the Reith Lectures. This is wrong. The Reith lectures were written in August 1963 and delivered in November, but the plan was finished on 28 December 1962. As already noted, there was no briefing document; the process was more intricate. Let us examine that process between 1 September and 28 December 1962. It consisted of intense dialogues between two professionals: a university professor and administrator and an architect. It is a bit like the last plate in Le Corbusier's *Urbanisme* which shows Louis XIV planning Les Invalides, with the caption '*Hommage à un grand urbaniste. Ce despot conçut des choses immenses et les realise.*'

The process consisted of Capon grilling Sloman about the Academic Plan. They had mutual influence, both of them, on the social plan. They 'walked and talked' the site. Finally the master plan came, out of a hat as a kind of Boxing Day present, completely unexpected. Sloman had anticipated something in brick, low-rise, maybe Anglo-Scandinavian, maybe neo-vernacular. He had no idea he was going to get a monumental complex.

As far as I can see, there were three key issues, all of which involved reconciling opposites. The first was size. Sloman wanted a very large university, but he also wanted a community. He wanted the thing to cohere. 10,000, perhaps 20,000 students. This was a time when the largest universities in Britain, Oxford and Cambridge, had 8,000 students. He had the prejudice against pavilions in the park and he wanted interdisciplinearity. Second, there was the park: landscaped, 130 acres, painted by Constable, an eighteenth-century villa rebuilt by Hopper in the late 1840s in a Dutch gable style, very fine; flat fields around the house which other architects had anticipated as the site of the campus; two dried up and muddy lakes; the site sloping down the valley towards the river on the west. Both Sloman and Capon wanted to retain the landscaped Park. Just below the towers you see part of the university teaching buildings which are sunk in the cleft of the valley. The third issue was that of the autonomous student flats and the Student Union.

Sloman, from his experience at Liverpool, appreciated that halls of residence, for which catering was a necessity, were extremely costly to operate. Second, he realised that students, even in the late Fifties, wanted their freedom. He also did not want the division between staff and students that arose from Senior Common Rooms and Student Unions. In other words, students should be independent of the Oxbridge conception of the university being *in loco parentis*. Yet oddly there were to be no places which students could call their own other than the flats.

Let's move to the key features of the campus. First, if the park were to be preserved, then very high density building was required. That sense community and interdisciplinearity also called for high density and communicability,

Figure 6. Square 4, 'the students will provide the ornament'

particularly between the teaching areas. Capon's solution was to create a high-density small city. I wouldn't call it either a megastructure or a building. It is a group of buildings, creating a great sense of intensity. It was also to be a 24-hour university. All facilities were to be on campus and all those 10–20,000 students were to be running around all hours of the day and night!

Originally it was to have had its own railway station. The land was actually bought, and then after an unfavourable UGC grant decision the land had to be sold again. It was to have car parking for up to 7.000 cars. Capon decided that you had to build in the valley, not on the level fields: a zig-zag net of offices, five to six storeys high, around enclosed squares, creating a high street – a central linked line of five pedestrian squares on raised concrete platforms with total traffic and pedestrian separation. Finally, there were to be twelve and fourteen-storey towers for the flats, slotted between the outer ends of the squares. There was to be minimal separation between different functions and a minimum of zoning.

The net of squares is unsurprising. It is well known that the highest density at the lowest cost is obtained with perimeter planning, which Leslie Martin and his Institute of Land Use Planning at Cambridge University was promoting at the time. Second, the Essex plan produced a system without distinct departmental pavilions; in fact the departments simply spread out along a continuous zig-zag of corridors that runs through the whole office area. As a result, departmental areas, communication between departments and flexibility are obtained. Third, administration, bars, restaurants, shops and teaching are completely unzoned, all mixed up with one another. Hence mixed uses. Fourth, it is a ten-minute walk from one edge of the campus to the other, that is, five minutes from the outer edge to the centre. Finally there are these five central squares forming the town centre in the form of a high street, creating a balance between enclosure and permeability. You can look through the suite of squares. A traditional, urban and collegiate form is employed such as one finds in Oxbridge, the Inns of Court, the London squares, or in Italian Renaissance cities. The question remains, why did the architects want such a traditional form? That's the easy part. But why did they want the towers? Essex was the only university to build towers.

As already noted, it was well known that high density flats are achievable with low-rise building. Capon knew this. Towers are also very expensive, and in fact the UGC declined to fund the Essex towers. Le Corbusier opposed very high-rise buildings for residential occupation. The university was set in landscaped parkland in Constable country on the Essex/Suffolk borders. The towers were a stumbling block with both the University Council and the University Grants Committee. But Capon was unyielding. The original model had 26 projected towers! He actually wanted eight. He got six. According to Sloman the arguments Capon used were that 'this is a form of dense development, a form we prefer because first, we think that the rooms with be very attractive with wonderful views over this marvellous park, and with low-rise you run the risk of spreading across this wonderful park.' In other words he pulled the wool over the eyes of the lay committees with the old fallacy that only high-rise could achieve high density. Sloman knew this, and he was convinced that Capon wanted the towers as a signal. I quote: 'he wanted to make this statement. Kenneth wanted to say, "that is the University of Essex, and it is important." There is a massiveness about the development, about the Library and the towers which brought out the strength and confidence of the university. It was going to be not just a local teaching institution but an institution which would have an international impact. The towers were part of this massiveness and strength. Kenneth and I were often using words like austerity, rigour, academic rigour. I think he felt that the towers helped to put across that message.'

I am sure that is part of the answer. But Christopher Townson, a former art history student who wrote his BA dissertation on the campus architecture, raised the issue in this form: 'Why didn't they use the towers for teaching? Why didn't they put the teaching or the library in towers that seem more appropriate?' Townson's explanation is first that large areas around the towers would have been required for lighting. The result would have been high-rise pavilions in the park which would have defeated one of Sloman's primary objectives. Second, with towers you have the problem of vertical communication between floors and departments, which would have destroyed another primary aim of the plan, that of creative intimacy and close ties between departments. The solution was to displace the symbolism from teaching to residential buildings.

But also I believe there was a neo-Corbusian, Team X rationale to this. High density, street and square for urbanism, and towers 'to retain the essential joys of sun, space and verdure.' I am quoting Peter Smithson here, in respect of Le Corbusier's 'l'espace, soleil, verdure.' Capon was truthful about wanting to retain the 'wonderful views'.

I will now turn to the context of the ideas that were in the air at this period. Mention of Team X leads to the question: what exactly was Capon up to? My original hunch was that the Essex campus was an example of the Corbusian contemporary city, but modified in the light of the attacks by Jane Jacobs and other pioneers of New Urbanism against rigid zoning, low densities, the destruction of the street. I am now convinced of this. Think of the key publications. 1957 – the Centre for Community Studies in Bethnal Green published Young and Willmott's *Family and Kinship in East London*. 1958 – *Fortune Magazine's* collection 'The Exploding Metropolis' published Jane Jacob's *Downtown is for People*, the first draft of her 1961 *Death and Life in Great American Cities*. In the same year, 1961, appeared Gordon Cullen's *Townscape* and Stirling and Gowan's interesting working class flats in Preston. Theo Crosby's *Uppercase Five* published Roger Mayne's photos of Bayham Street. In December 1962 *Architectural Design*, of which Crosby and Kenneth Frampton were editors, published the *Team X Primer*, their manifesto developed over the preceding decade.

In the eighteen months before work on the Essex master plan began there was deep concern, both within the architectural profession and amongst the general public, about the previous decade of post-war reconstruction. Festival of Britain, new towns, all that low-density stuff, overspill estates, Anglo-Scandinavian vernacular, the destruction of the Victorian cityscape, the

Figure 7. Bayham Street by Roger Mayne, from *Uppercase 5*, 1961

suburbanisation of the city as Raymond Erith called it, came into sharp focus in a series of books, manifestos, buildings and major demolitions such as that of the Euston Arch.

If architects were dismayed by the gutlessness of the low-density, suburban, picturesque garden city and garden suburb character of much recent public housing and urban planning, the burden of Young and Willmott's 1957 critique of post-war slum clearance, decanting and dispersal (surely an influence upon Jane Jacobs) was that the destruction of the nineteenth-century bye-law street brought with it the destruction of the tight-knit, self-supporting, working-class community, resulting in the anomie of the overspill estates.

Jacobs developed this into an explicit critique of functional zoning. She sang the virtues of the old inner-city slums, of mixed uses, community surveillance, the 24-hour city, the organic lively city represented in the work of US photographers such as Weegee, Bill Klein, and the young Robert Rauschenberg as well as that of British photographers like Mayne and Henderson and of the new generation of working class novelists. What was developing, at the very moment it was being swept away or gentrified, was a deep *nostalgie de boue*, nostalgia of the slums.

Thus the significance of Roger Mayne's photos of kids playing in Victorian, run-down streets in Kensal Green, North Kensington. Thus Stirling and Gowan on their little-known, high-density, street-hugging courtyard scheme in Preston in 1961, about which they wrote, 'the nineteenth-century industrial town is justly condemned as being inadequate in standards of health. Nevertheless there exists a neighbourliness and communal vitality which is quite absent in the present-day solutions: the suburban dilution of the garden city coupled with 'contemporary' style … We hope to perpetuate a familiar and vital environment.'

The means for recreating the rugged vitality of the Victorian city was the street. The cry was 'back to the bye-law street', anathema to 1930s modernists. The Smithsons proclaimed, 'In the bye-law streets there is an inherent feeling of safety and social bond which has much to do with the obviousness and simple form of the street.' The street, like the other components of traditional towns and cities, the square, the village green, the boulevard, was believed to be a timeless constant in urban architecture, because it reflected a constant in human nature and society. Of course, it was the *concept* of the street, not its traditional shape and form, that was important to Team X. Central to this concern for the timeless traditional urban forms or typologies was Team X's sense of the crucial importance of public enclosure, of the spaces between buildings 'both to define these negative spaces positively as outdoor rooms and passageways, and through that to recreate a sense of place.' (Peter Smithson).

Aldo van Eyck wrote, 'Architects have expelled all sense of place, have created no-places with their flat, unsculpted, germ-free surfaces. Architecture should be making good places particularly for children. And the good city should be a bunch of places.' There is a clear Heideggerian echo when Van Eyck proclaims 'Architecture can assist man's homecoming.' Of course this also lay at the heart of Cullen's *Townscape* with its stress upon place, precinct, closure, enclosure, and that very Heideggerian word, thereness.

Turning finally to architectural style, somewhat less important to these people than urbanism, they hated the gutlessness of so-called 'Contemporary Architecture' – Festival of Britain, neo-vernacular and high-tech. They liked the poetry of Le Corbusier. If the spirit of a real city, its vitality and energy, were to be created or preserved, that poetry would of necessity be sublime rather than beautiful.

These are some of the ideas that were in the air. I don't know for sure how Capon or ACP responded to them. Sadly, most of the founding partners are now dead. But to judge from the appearance and urban form of the Essex University campus, they must have absorbed them. A key statement of Capon's is recalled by Sloman. 'The buildings are unadorned because the students will provide the ornament.' That's very much in the spirit, I think, of those photographs by Roger Mayne.

So how did it work out in practice? The Essex campus is an academic city not a building. The master plan combined three typologies: the city, particularly the Italian Renaissance city; the medieval university, or Inns of Court, with its squares and courts; and Plato's Academy, the academic grove and the park. The key thing was to create the urban fabric for an academic community, in which learning, administration, eating, drinking, shopping, sociability, and accommodation all took place close to one another and overlapped to create a convivial spirit. Had the target population of 10,000 been reached, a critical mass for all those bars, a 24-hour university city would have been achieved.

The spinal high street of five squares and the medieval maze of internal corridors, which bewilders newcomers, have the result that one is always bumping into people from other departments – particularly when one gets lost, as I still do after almost thirty years. The plan does create sociability. The loggias, cloisters and squares, south facing to catch the sun, create a strong sense of enclosure and possess a somewhat monastic austerity, traditionally appropriate to universities. And then there are the internal courtyards, gardens, quieter places for contemplation, one of which formed an outdoor theatre, with a beautiful loggia which has sadly been filled in recently for offices. The major civic monuments are also dispersed through the fabric: the library, the restaurants, the lecture theatres designed by Jim Cadbury-Brown.

The density and compactness of this city does indeed mean that the park is preserved, just like the Cambridge backs or Christchurch Meadow. The buildings of the campus are seen across parkland and through screens of trees.

Finally the towers. No, not essential to preserve the park, not dreaming spires. But a signal, yes. They establish the university upon the skyline, much as the towers of nearby Ely established that community upon the Fens. The Essex towers are built of solid structural brickwork without a frame, using grey engineering brick for its load-bearing strength, emulating Burnham and Root's 1891 Monadnock Building in Chicago. The Essex towers are designed with great subtlety, and present an infinite variety of groupings from all the different points of view around the campus. They cluster together like a castle, they line up in futuristic skyscraper canyons, they mass together like cliffs. I'm not sure exactly what they signify or suggest. In fact, I can only really appeal to Edmund Burke and John Ruskin: 'A severe and mysterious majesty, an undiminished awe like that felt at the presence and operation of some great spiritual power.' The towers are not beautiful, precious, certainly not delicate, though detailed with exquisite care, but majestic, awe-inspiring and even somewhat fearsome.

The towers also bear a resemblance to Giles Gilbert Scott's great Library tower at Cambridge – note the detailing of the windows, the way that the windows form continuous vertical lines with the brick piers between them. Perhaps there was some association emblematic of the dedication to scaling the heights of scholarship, so much in the minds of Sloman and Capon in their walks about the park in the autumn of 1962 as they discussed the idea of a university for the modern age. Perhaps the Essex towers sound a similar note of gravity to Scott's tower, framed as it once was by his Memorial Court at Clare College until Philip Dowson's act of desecration blocked that sombre vista built in memory to the young men who fell in the Great War, on the frivolous grounds (I quote from Dowson's document) that the view was 'somewhat oppressive'.

One of the characteristics of great architecture is its capacity to move one at a pre-verbal level, to suggest uncomfortable thoughts and feelings without

Figure 8. Loggia in Theatre courtyard, now filled in

Figure 9. Park and towers from
Wivenhoe Park

meeting the resistance which would arise in response to those ideas being
stated in words or in obvious symbols. Architecture is most often experienced,
as Walter Benjamin put it, in a state of distraction, not in a state of concentrated perception. At the same age as present-day students go to university,
Sloman had himself been a fighter pilot. Remember, too, that this was the
height of the Campaign for Nuclear Disarmament, the time of the Cuban
Missile Crisis and that in 1962 the 90-year-old Bertrand Russell had been ar-
rested for sitting in Whitehall as part of a Committee of One Hundred protest
against nuclear weapons. Peter Smithson has said he remembers it was 6 June
1964 when the Economist Building was opened because it was D-Day. I suggest
that these Essex towers are, in some way, war memorials. Since antiquity the
tower has been employed as a memorial. I would also argue that the new universities of the 1960s should be regarded as manifestations of the final stage of
post-war reconstruction.

In general, the university functions very well in practical terms. Staff and
students praise its compactness, the squares, the library, the park. I readily

Figure 10. North Towers

Figure 11. Skyscraper canyons

admit, however, that people do not by and large find it attractive aesthetically. They condemn the grey concrete, the dark grey brickwork of the towers, the absence of ornament. But this is to misunderstand the type of architecture which it represents. It was built by the light of Ruskin's Lamp of Power, not his Lamp of Beauty, though of course it is set in the natural beauty of Wivenhoe Park. It is an example of the architectural sublime – appropriately so, as I have tried to suggest, for an institution which stands firmly in the traditions of Plato's Academy, as well as seeking to remind 'the young in one another's arms' of graver matters. And I personally believe that it will be recognised as one of the masterpieces of twentieth-century architecture and urbanism, and will be included in the great tradition of British architecture and town planning, the Georgian townscape, and Victorian civic monuments.

Finally, I promised in my introduction to explain the connection between the New Urbanism associated with the Prince of Wales, the return to the form of the traditional city, and the Essex campus.

The architecture and urbanism of the 1960s remains unpopular with the general public. Condemned as 'modernist' its products are seen as brutalist, grey, functional, collectivist, soul-destroying and totalitarian. But in my view this architecture was not 'modernist. The late 1950s and 1960s marked the end of modernism in art and architecture alike. Modernism had its origins in the 1870s, flowered between 1905 and 1930, but because of the war it did not become establishment orthodoxy till after 1945, coming to a climax in the early 1960s with the destruction of the London skyline and other phenomena of that period. This periodicisation of modernism is loosely based upon Bernard Smith's *Modernism's History* of 1998. Modernism has been confused with Counter-Modernism.

Counter-Modernism had its origins in the Dada and Surrealism of the 1920s. Insofar as it related to architecture the key text was Louis Aragon's *Paysan de Paris* (Paris Peasant) of 1924 and 1925 describing the author's highly imaginative experience of the everyday low-life community of the Passage de l'Opéra in Paris, just about to be demolished for the last of Haussmann's boulevards. This approach to life in the city came to fruition in the cluster of ideas I mentioned earlier: anti-zoning, community, the timeless traditions of human place-making, the street and the home, the threshold, conservationism and historical revival, and praise for the great unplanned cities of the free

Figure 12. Lecture theatres by H.T.
Cadbury-Brown, with south towers
behind. (Steve Cole, National
Monuments Record, English Heritage)

market west coast of the USA such as Los Angeles and Las Vegas. Essex, the
24-hour university city of 20,000 students with its 26 skyscrapers was one of the
first products of this new ethos. Like the work of Team X itself, the Essex
campus was, however, transitional. It does not break altogether with the architectural language of modernism.

Two of the architectural thinkers of the 1970s and 1980s who were most
influential upon New Urbanism and upon the ideas of the Prince of Wales
sprang from the same roots. Leon Krier had worked for Jim Stirling; like the
members of Team X he had been a great admirer of Le Corbusier in his youth
and only subsquently turned to the classical language of architecture. His 1978
manifesto *The Reconstruction of the European City* exhibits a direct debt to the
ideas of the early 1960s. The same is true of Christopher Alexander's *A Pattern
Language* of 1977 and his *The Timeless Way of Building*, 1979.

One of Krier's key ideas is that in cities such as Florence or Siena one can
walk from end to end of the Renaissance centre in ten minutes. It is no accident
or coincidence that it takes just ten minutes to walk from one end of the Essex
campus to the other, and it takes only five minutes for a student to get from
their bedroom in one of the towers to the lecture room.

11 | The Brutal Birth of Archigram

SIMON SADLER

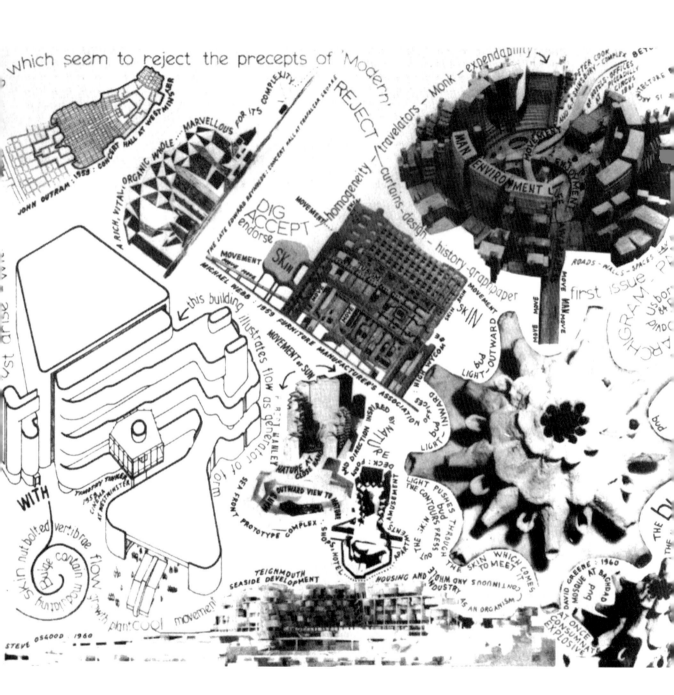

which seem to reject the precepts of 'Modern,'

JOHN OUTRAM : 1959 : CONCERT HALL AT WESTMINSTER

A RICH, VITAL, ORGANIC WHOLE... MARVELLOUS FOR ITS COMPLEXITY...

THE LATE EDWARD REYNOLDS : CONCERT HALL AT TRAFALGAR SQUARE

'REJECT
travelators - Monk - expendability
homogeneity
curtains - design - history - graph paper

DIG
ACCEPT
endorse

MOVEMENT
SKIN

MICHAEL WEBB : 1959 FURNITURE MANUFACTURER'S ASSOCIATION

this building illustrates MOVEMENT of SUN flow as generator of form

TIMOTHY TINKER 1958 CINEMA AT WESTMINSTER

WITH

Bulge contain modulating SKIN nut bolted vertibrae flow growth plant COOL movement

STEVE OSGOOD 1960

TEIGNMOUTH SEASIDE DEVELOPMENT

NATURE AT CLOSE RANGE

MAIN OUTWARD VIEW TO NATURE

SEA FRONT PROTOTYPE COMPLEX

AND DIRECTION INSPIRED BY NATURE

DECK : PORT

SHOPS HOTEL

APARTMENTS

THE WK AMUSEMENTS

MAN ENVIRONMENT

MOVEMENT

first issue

ROADS - WALLS - SPACES

SKIN

bud LIGHT - OUTWARD

LIGHT - INWARD

LIGHT pushes THROUGH THE bud THE CONTOURS PRESS OUT

SKIN WHICH COMES TO MEET IT

CONTINUOUS AND WHOLE AS AN ORGANISM

HOUSING AND INDUSTRY

DAVID GREENE 1960 MOSQUE AT BAGHDAD

bud

AT ONCE CONSUMMATE EXPLOSIVE

THE bud

bud

The Brutal Birth of Archigram

SIMON SADLER

Archigram, the group with a little magazine that became the preeminent architectural avant-garde of the 1960s, was a youthful flowering of ideas that had been current on the fringes of competitions and discussion groups. 'All of us were lucky because it was something waiting to happen', Michael Webb has said of the Archigram phenomenon. 'We came at a time (1961) when there was a lot of architectural territory to move into and the work flowed out of us. For a generation immediately after us we had usurped all their architectural land.'[1] The territory was left vacant by the transition of the Brutalists, Britain's previous architectural vanguard, into the sort of classical respectability embodied by Alison and Peter Smithson's Economist Building, London (1960–64). Before it became famous for designing scandalous Walking Cities and Living Pods, Archigram started out as a sort of second wave Brutalism, pushing Brutalism's formal and technical possibilities to the limit.

The first *Archigram* was printed by Gestetner on two sheets and distributed in 1961 via London's Architectural Association (AA) and Regent Street Polytechnic to anyone prepared to shell-out 'the grand price of 6d and 1/6'[2] – mainly students and newly graduated professionals.[3] It was created by an extended group of contributors, before its core membership of just six men became established in 1963 with the publication of *Archigram* no.3. Two of those members, Peter Cook and David Greene (the former from the AA, the latter hailing from Nottingham School of Architecture) made the selections for the first edition, conscripting a third member, Michael Webb, from the Architectural Association's arch rival, the Regent Street Polytechnic. They were outspoken students enjoying 'famous' school careers, none more so than Webb. At the time that Webb's 1957–8 student project for a new Furniture Manufacturer's Building in High Wycombe was being exhibited at the Museum of Modern Art

Figure 1. Main spread of *Archigram* no.1, May 1961

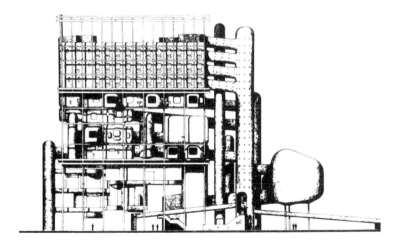

Figure 2. Michael Webb, Furniture Manufacturers Association Building in High Wycombe project, elevation (Regent Street Polytechnic fourth-year, 1957–8)

1. Michael Webb, interview with Herbert Lachmayer and Pascal Schöning at The Russell Hotel, London, 13/12/1991.

2. Letter to the author from Roy Payne, 12 May 1998. Payne was studying at the Regent Street Polytechnic between 1960 and 1966, and helped sell the magazine.

3. Interview with Gordon Sainsbury, Cambridge, Mass., 27/4/98.

in New York, Nikolaus Pevsner was moved to contrast the generally 'promis-ing' state of British architecture with student work,[4] dismissing it as an attempt to 'out-Gaudí Gaudí'.[5] 'What will happen with students', asked Reyner Banham in his rejoinder to Pevsner, 'when what they see in their history lectures is stronger and tougher stuff than they get taught in their studio in-struction? What happens when the practising masters of the day produce only near-beer, and the slides that are shown in the history lectures are 80° proof?'[6] With this, Banham was inciting a return to the avant-garde origins of modern architecture, mapped out in his *Theory and Design in the First Machine Age* of 1960.

Launched at just the moment when Brutalism was slipping down a gear into the municipal, *Archigram* was perfectly in the logic of the avant-garde and of student agitation. Michael Webb knew the value of this sort of agitation, having been involved in the Regent Street Polytechnic's architectural magazine *Polygon*. Though never as radical as *Archigram*, the magazine enjoyed an 'avid student readership',[7] and the impact of its first couple of editions upon the stirrings at the Architectural Association was 'critical',[8] im-ported by its editors Wilfred Marden and John Outram when they transferred to the AA for their fourth years, the latter contributing to *Archigram*. *Polygon* fed into the student restlessness that had become apparent in the formation of the British Architectural Students Association (BASA) in 1958,[9] representing twenty-five schools and destined to become a sparring partner of Archigram.

'*Archigram* 1 was an outburst against the sterility of architecture surround-ing one in London in the winter of 1960–61', *Architectural Design* explained in 1965.[10] Looking for inspiration, 'student work of the mid-fifties was all that could be pointed to'. Eight recent projects, all exploring 'post-Brutalist' possibilities, were stuffed on to that first *Archigram* broadsheet, a collage of meandering images and words. The late Edward Reynolds's project for a Concert Hall at Trafalgar Square acted as something of a talisman, an exemplar of the 'virtuoso free-forming at the AA'.[11] Reynolds's 'cubist' handling of form facetted every surface of the project, shown at the 1957 AA student exhibition which was lauded for its 'breakaway from graphpaper':[12] it seemed to AA tutor and Brutalist architect William Howell that the new work marked 'both an intellectual and a poetic reaction against the straight-up-and-down, strictly rectangular, tee-square and set-square, exposed frame structure'.[13]

'THIS IS ARCHIGRAM – PAPER ONE – A STATEMENT', the cover announced, though it took more than a little effort on the part of the reader to piece the 'statement' together. Words fell about so that they would be read synchro-nously, snaking around the page as if their sum meanings were so outrageous to the early sixties design establishment that they should be subject to a controlled release, intelligible only to those who were appropriately youthful:

A new generation of architecture must arise – with forms and spaces that seem to reject the precepts of 'Modern'
REJECT – curtains – design – history – graph paper
DIG ACCEPT endorse – homogeneity – travelators – Monk – expendability

The rejection of 'design' was a traumatic request for architects, and surprising given Archigram's subsequently massive production of drawings. But there it was: design, as in the cut-and-dried presentation of a solution, was too static, premeditated and removed from environmental context to be literally tran-scribed into built form; there can therefore be no more design in the traditional sense of the word. The determinism of orthogonals, or the logic of the studio-produced statistical 'graph' as a source for environmental control had to go the same way; the jibe was aimed at the sort of rationalist / Modernist teaching at the key schools (part of the first year at the Bartlett, for instance, was spent studying science and a choice of 'allometry, semiotics, Markovian analysis, sensory thresholds, self-regulating systems, Boolean algebra, theory of

4. Michael Webb, lecture at the Bartlett School of Architecture, London, 22/3/98.

5. Nikolaus Pevsner, 'Modern Architecture and the Historian, or, the Return of Historicism', *RIBA Journal*, April 1961, pp.230–240, p.231, cited in Jonathan Hughes, '1961', in Louise Campbell, ed., *Twentieth-Century Architecture and its Histories*, London: Society of Architectural Historians of Great Britain, 2001.

6. Pevsner, 'Modern Architecture and the Historian', p.238, cited in Hughes, '1961', ibid.

7. Brian Hanson, 'Polygon', in *Rassegna (Architecture in the Little Magazines)*, vol.4, no.12, Milan, December 1982, p.72.

8. Peter Cook, 'The Electric Decade: An Atmosphere at the AA School 1963–73', in James Gowan, ed., *A Continuing Experiment: Learning and Teaching at the Architectural Association*, London, Architectural Press, 1975, pp.137–146, p.138, ftn 3.

9. See George Kassaboff, John Outram, Paul Power, Ian McKechnie, 'Student Section – BASA', *Architects' Journal*, vol.129, no.3342, 19 March 1959, p.451.

10. Anon., 'Archigram Group, London: A chronological survey', *Architectural Design*, vol.35, no.11, November 1965, p.560.

11. ibid. Reynolds died in 1959.

12. *Archigram* no.1, London 1961, n.p.

13. William Howell, writing in the *AA Journal* vol.74, February 1959, p.218, quoted in Brian Hanson, "Il momento inglese", *Rassegna (Architecture in the Little Magazines)*, vol.4, no.12, Milan, December 1982, pp.31–40.

measurement or the theory of limits').[14] In place of such high-sounding approaches Archigram proposed Futurist 'expendability', a permit to do away with designs as soon as their peak of efficiency has passed.

The new architecture should 'seem to reject precepts of the Modern' – the precepts taught in the architectural schools, perhaps, though not necessarily the precepts of the Modernist pioneers. *Archigram* no.1 announced 'WE HAVE CHOSEN TO BYPASS THE DECAYING BAUHAUS IMAGE WHICH IS AN INSULT TO FUNCTIONALISM', including the ubiquitous motif of the curtain wall. Instead of the *image* of standardisation presented by the curtain wall, true 'homogeneity' would return architecture to its dream of standardised, mass-produced structures that could be deployed *ad hoc*. The spirit of the machine age would live again, its citizens transported by travelator. These young architects sought the uncorrupted source of an ethos which had whetted their appetites for experimentation, technology and structure.

Like Henry Ford, the Modern Movement had largely rejected 'history', at least in its more obvious deference to the Orders, decoration, symmetry and hierarchical typologies. Yet it had retained others, particularly proportion, trabeation and axial planning – one only had to look at the temples in Le Corbusier's *Vers une architecture*, or John Summerson's final chapter of *The Classical Language of Architecture* (1963), or to Banham's examination of the Beaux-Arts origins of certain Modernist axioms in the first chapter of *Theory and Design in the First Machine Age*. The Archigram generation of architects would not submit to the classical pattern-book. New buildings would be placed on top of and around those existing buildings whose fixed plans had out-served their usefulness. The result would be architectural disjunction, a visual break with yesterday, an anti-idealism. Architecture would embrace discord, like jazz pianist renegade Thelonious Monk, and would adopt the same choppy, streetwise tone in which *Archigram*'s statement was scripted.[15]

As the Economist Building showed, not even Brutalism had achieved the escape velocity needed to pull out of the classical orbit. In their student projects Webb, Cook and Greene dared to turn the logic of the New Brutalism in upon itself. If Brutalism – the most challenging style of British architecture in the Fifties – still wanted a frank exposure of process, of circulation, of response, and a sensitivity to site and technology, Archigram would carry on meting it out, in spades. The departure point of the youngsters, visible in *Archigram* no.1, was a 'topology' (to use a word in vogue in the Fifties) gone mad: an obsessive interest in circulation; in a complex, 'organic' relationship to site; in a 'rational' separation and expression of services; even in a compositional formlessness derived from Abstract Expressionism and *art brut*. Allied to Pier Luigi Nervi's in-situ ferrocimento method, with an exoskeleton holding pre-cast floor panels, Webb's Furniture Manufacturer's Building showed how far the principles could be pushed, and the results were, if anything, too avant-garde, a 'cartoon architecture' too flashy to qualify as Brutalism.[16] The frame valiantly imposed a visual order to volumes on the brink of formlessness, swallowing up a showroom and company offices on the lower floors, lettable office space in attic storeys, with a bulbous auditorium clinging to the side through umbilical cords. One could legitimately expose the services, like the water tower at the Brutalist icon of Hunstanton Secondary School (Alison and Peter Smithson, 1949–54). But a building like the Furniture Manufacturer's that was apparently nothing *but* services, stacked crazily in a frame, lacked decorum. And the expression of circulation in it temporarily defied categorisation: Reyner Banham, who had discovered the term 'topological' for the Smithsons, had to rise to the challenge again when he declared the explosion of work at Regent Street Polytechnic to be 'Bowellist'. If 'topology' had attempted to relate the building to principles derived from geographical layout and abstract mathematics, 'Bowellism' related the building to the

14. Crinson & Lubbock, *Architecture, Art or Profession?: three hundred years of architectural education in Britain*, Manchester, Manchester University Press, 1994, p.148, citing Richard Llewelyn Davies, *The Education of an Architect*, London, 1961, p.6, and Dean Latourell, 'The Bartlett 1969', *AIA Journal*, October 1969, p.91.

15. Christopher Booker, *The Neophiliacs: a study of the revolution in English life in the Fifties and Sixties*, London, Collins, 1969, p.41. 'DIG', in case the reader of *Archigram* didn't realise, meant 'endorse' (in *The Neophiliacs*, a critical survey of the 1960s published eight years later, the conservative Christopher Booker wearily explained that the embrace both of jazz and sensational language signified the 'almost indefinable state of being "hep" [*sic*] or "in the groove."')

16. See Appleyard, *Richard Rogers – a biography*, London and Boston, Faber, 1986, p.181: 'To the Smithsons it was Mickey Mouse architecture …'.

circulation of the gut and to biological systems, announced in its disturbing, bulbous forms.

Biology and technology, only metaphors for the Brutalists, were models for Archigram. Greene took the cue in his startling 1961 Seaside Entertainments Building, its main chambers hovering translucent like the muscles of a heart from an aorta service tower. The implication was that the Seaside Building could comfortably become part of a larger architectural / biological machine. Again, in Cook's Car Body / Pressed Metal Cabin student housing project of 1961–2, there seemed to be something too *literal* about the design, in this case a transcription of enthusiasms for industrial design that were expected in Brutalist circles to be tempered by an instinct for 'proper' architecture. Archigram tried to show that 'Detroit-styled' houses were not a proposition for twenty-five years' hence (as the Smithsons were at pains to claim in regard to their famous 'Pop' House of the Future for the 1956 *Ideal Home* Exhibition), but for the here-and-now of the 1960s, thus questioning Brutalism's increasing austerity and concrete fixity.

Webb, Greene and Cook had got to know each other in 1959 'and used to meet up pretty regularly in a "greasy spoon" caff at Swiss Cottage'.[17] Cook noticed the competition entries being submitted by London County Council (LCC) employees Ron Herron, Dennis Crompton and Warren Chalk, and he invited them to contribute to the second edition of *Archigram* in 1962, lending it a professional credibility that it might have lacked had it continued as a student rag. 'Crazy stuff', Cook recalled of the competition entries from the LCC set,[18] though it would be more accurate to say that the LCC work represented the cutting-edge of what the new wave of Brutalism could realistically hope to get built. Able to take advantage of their relative freedom as recent graduates, Cook, Greene and Webb had been cultivating work that was more romantic than that of their colleagues working in the real-world grind of the LCC. This became evident when teams from both of Archigram's pools, 'graduate' and 'LCC', entered the 1961 Lincoln Civic Centre Competition. The Chalk, Herron and Crompton entry, which gained a commendation, was in the 'late Brutalist' style that they were deploying at the LCC's South Bank project: a 'topological' plan, incorporating any number of irregular polygonal shapes, stacked in elevation over several levels, pulled together by a few deftly-placed walkways. Contrasting with the hard-edge approach of the LCC team were Cook and Greene's more Bowellist, soft, poetic, low-rise elevations, hugging a landscaped site.[19] Yet common to both entries was a love of mound-like buildings, which would emerge as a key theme in the work of the Archigram group.

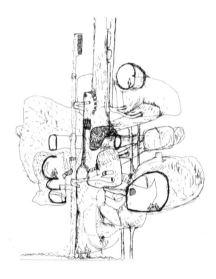

Figure 3. David Greene, Seaside Entertainments Building project (Cliffside Entertainments Building), drawing, 1961

Figure 4. Peter Cook, Car Body / Pressed Metal Cabin student housing project, plan and elevation, 1961–2

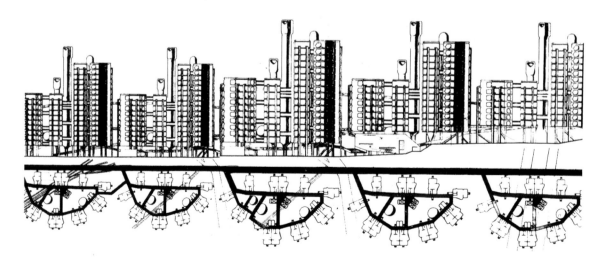

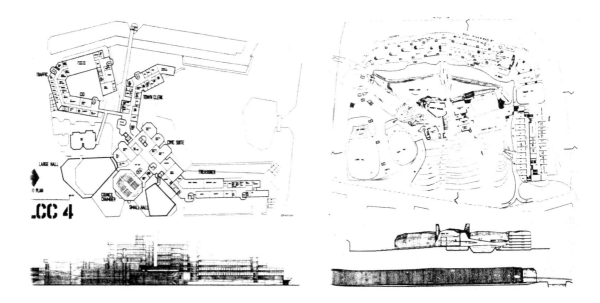

Ron Herron had joined the LCC's Schools Division in 1954. The LCC had previously employed the Brutalist architects whose influence on the nascent Archigram was so evident; Alison and Peter Smithson themselves had briefly worked in the Schools Division, partly using the time to complete work on Hunstanton Secondary School.[20] It was at the LCC that Herron met Warren Chalk, who joined the same year, and they become inseparable – 'the Morecambe and Wise of architecture'.[21] Chalk and Herron's designs between 1956 and 1958 – their Paisley Technical College and Enfield Civic Centre competition entries, and Chalk's Chelsea College of Advanced Education – were competent if modest combinations of 1920s Corbusian styling and a certain Brutalist ruggedness. Even Herron's more widely noticed 1957 St. Pancras Starcross (Prospect) Secondary School, with Peter Nicholls, had as many fashionable similarities with the old as with the new. In 1968 Roy Landau singled it out as an exemplar of young LCC architecture. In Landau's concise description, Starcross 'was a Modern-Movement, classically grouped building complex with Garches-smooth facades'; on the other hand, 'it had the current vernacular inverted-L window and used a "movement organising" concourse bridge, an idea of the Brutalists.'[22]

It was a start for the young pretenders, at least, and it found its way into select company in G.E. Kidder-Smith's *The New Architecture of Europe*, pub-

Figure 5. (left) Chalk, Herron and Crompton (with John Attenborough, Terry Kennedy, John Roberts, Alan Waterhouse), Lincoln Civic Centre Competition, plan and elevation, 1961; (right): Cook and Greene, Lincoln Civic Centre Competition, plan and elevation, 1961

Figure 6. Ron Herron and Peter Nicholls for London County Council, Starcross (Prospect) Secondary School, St. Pancras, London 1957

17. Cook, 'A Quickstart Introduction to the Archigram Group', in Archigram, ed., *A Guide to Archigram 1961–74*, London, Academy, 1994, p.6.

18. ibid., p.8.

19. The Cook / Greene entry for the Berkshire County Offices Competition the following year was a comparable achievement.

20. See Anthony Jackson, *The Politics of Architecture: a history of modern architecture in Britain*, London, Architectural Press, 1970, p.194.

21. Norman Engleback, address to the 20th Century Society's Hayward Gallery symposium, Architectural Association, London 20/3/99.

22. Royston Landau, *New Directions in British Architecture*, London, Studio Vista, 1968, p.46.

Figure 7. Chalk, Herron, Crompton, and John Attenborough, for group leader Norman Engleback at the Special Works Division of the LCC, South Bank Arts Centre, 1960–67, seen from the pedestrian deck to the south-west

lished by Penguin in 1961. Some features of the Starcross school foretold the increasingly radical LCC work that Herron would be involved in at the South Bank Centre. For instance, Starcross was designed with the facility to be enlarged and changed (into a college), much as the South Bank would be, anticipating the architecture of endless 'becoming' that would preoccupy Archigram. The uses of a multi-level plan at Starcross were striking. Herron and Nicholl took to heart Brutalist ideas of circulation and multiple function, borrowed from the Smithsons and Aldo van Eyck. In addition to the '"movement-organising" concourse bridge' that caught Landau's eye at Starcross, Kidder Smith noted that 'by excavating and clearing the basements of the houses previously on the site, a sunken playground, which flows right under the east end of the elevated teaching block, was created so that outdoor recreation could be enjoyed even in bad weather,'[23] a foretaste of the South Bank's infamous undercroft. So it was that ideas about multi-level deck access, independent systems of movement, the principle of 'cluster' and, for that matter, *béton brut*, began to be properly realised not so much under the Brutalist 'avant-garde' itself, but under a 'retardataire' of architects at the LCC. Warren Chalk, the eldest member of the group, admitted that he could have fallen in with the earlier camp of Brutalists – 'I joined your lot. I could have joined the other lot.'[24]

Chalk and Herron encountered Dennis Crompton when, upon recommendation from a friend, they persuaded him in 1960 to leave Frederick Gibberd's office for the glamorous LCC Special Works Division, to which they had been transferred.[25] Together, their South Bank complex would be a snapshot of advanced architectural interests at the turn of the new decade. Under Chalk, Herron, Crompton, and John Attenborough, for group leader Norman Engleback, the South Bank Arts Centre finally juxtaposed the New Brutalism with the great achievement of an earlier generation of British Modernists, the Royal Festival Hall (1948–51), which was being remodelled at the same time. Contrary to the Festival Hall's bright, civic, slightly nautical and unerringly rational confidence, the South Bank Centre truculently crumbled its two shuttered-concrete concert-halls and gallery into the riverside, deflecting any hint of a processional route with blind bends and furtive staircases, reluctant to reveal so much as a front door.

Though powerfully sculptural, the Centre's resistance to being a resolved composition is underlined when compared to its superficially similar Cubist neighbour on the other side, Denys Lasdun's National Theatre (1967–77), which is held in check by its regulating horizontal layers and crisp corners. Critics and admirers alike soon noted the expressionism of the South Bank Centre.[26] Debts to the 1920s, to Le Corbusier and Konstantin Melnikov, even to Rudolf Steiner could be detected, but in a state too dreamlike to be nailed

23. G.E. Kidder Smith, *The New Architecture of Europe*, Harmondsworth, Penguin, 1962, p.52.

24. Peter Cook, address to the AA 150 Anniversary seminar at the Clore Management Centre, Birkbeck College, London, 9/7/97.

25. Anon., 'Archigram Group, London: A chronological survey', *Architectural Design*, vol.35, no.11, November 1965, p.560.

26. See Landau, *New Directions in British Architecture*, pp.31–37.

down as straight historical antecedents (with odd exceptions like the Unité d'Habitation-derived staircase on the Queen Elizabeth Hall). Imagery was potent but abstract, the silhouette bristling with pyramid skylights, the Hayward's west window like a pill-box gun installation or visor, the aggression of the whole ensemble tempered by a comic-book eclecticism of the sort that would be found in *Archigram* no.4, 1964.

A lugubrious project – first designed in 1960, completed in 1964, and officially opened in 1967 – the strange massing of the South Bank explored several interests central to Archigram's architecture. The first was its adaptation of the pedestrian net devised by the Smithsons in their 1957 Berlin Haupstadt project: the South Bank Centre was the first serious attempt to build the Brutalist multi-level city, with the ravines of imaginary vehicular traffic separated from pedestrian circulation above. The building seemed to have a disproportionate amount of 'exterior', solving at the same time the classic design problem of articulating the blank elevation of an auditorium. Unlike Berlin Haupstadt, though, the South Bank's 'topological' walkways purported to connect one place to another rather than provide an abstract sense of mobility: Chalk was assigned to design the walkways and approaches to the Centre,[27] one rationale being the hope that British Rail would build an escalator link from Waterloo station.[28] The building took further cues from the walkways of Sheffield's famous Park Hill estate (Lewis Womersley, Jack Lynn and Ivor Smith, 1953–59), and from the surface textures of surrounding buildings too: John Miller and Christopher Dean's Brutalist Old Vic Theatre workshops (1957–8, for Lyons Israel Ellis), and Owen Williams's Sainsbury's warehouse in Stamford Street.[29]

Figure 8. Pedestrian deck intersection of the South Bank Centre, 1960–67, with the Royal Festival Hall, 1948–51/62

But of course the circulation plan of the South Bank Centre was far from being a functionalist exercise. Extruding a new pedestrian deck from the Festival Hall's terrace level, the South Bank Centre wilfully heaped-up into a miniature multi-level 'city'. As Edward Jones and Christopher Woodward have acerbically noted, in the event 'the raised pedestrian decks and bridges seem both inconvenient and irrelevant on this quiet site, with no through traffic from which pedestrians might need protection. The decks are windy, offering no protection from the weather, and are difficult for the frail or disabled to negotiate.'[30] It is a criticism that benefits from hindsight, and the adventure of visiting the complex has since been curtailed by blocked staircases and closed terraces, sacrificed to cheap crime prevention and the vicissitudes of architectural fashion. Nonetheless the South Bank Centre's insensitivity to the infirm betrayed its Futurist inspirations, prioritising the young and able-bodied, motorised vehicles, and air, with ducts heroically scaled and standing proud of the volumes of the building.[31]

'The original basic concept', Chalk recalled in 1966, 'was to produce an anonymous pile, subservient to a series of pedestrian walkways, a sort of Mappin Terrace [the artificial mountain at London Zoo] for people instead of goats.'[32] The exposure of pedestrians to wind and wet as they hike along the bridges, ridges and plateaux of the South Bank emphasised the designers' preoccupation with styling the building as some sort of natural or organic feature. The agglomeration of sheer cliffs of shuttered wood-grained concrete, contrasting with the overscaled rock-like rounded deck walls, alluded to geology and weathering, and in Archigram's self-penned 1971 anthology, the South Bank Centre was covered in a discussion of the group's fascination with 'mounds' and 'crusts' (themes examined in *Archigram* no.5, 1964). One drawing by Herron even proposed turfing over the entire structure.[33] And so the nearest Archigram came to major built statements began and ended with the metaphor of the mound, of the disappeared building: the still-born Monte Carlo Entertainments Centre (1969–73) was to have been built literally beneath a mound.

27. Norman Engleback, address to the 20th Century Society's Hayward Gallery symposium, Architectural Association, London 20/3/99.

28. Robert Maxwell, address to the 20th Century Society's Hayward Gallery symposium, Architectural Association, London 20/3/99.

29. Andrew Saint, address to the 20th Century Society's Hayward Gallery symposium, Architectural Association, London 20/3/99.

30. Edward Jones & Christopher Woodward, *A Guide to the Architecture of London*, 2nd edition, London, Weidenfeld and Nicholson, 1992, p.258.

31. For commentary on the Queen Elizabeth Hall's services, see Reyner Banham, *The Architecture of the Well-tempered Environment*, London, Architectural Press, 1969, pp.255–64.

32. Warren Chalk, 'Architecture as consumer product', *Arena: the Architectural Association Journal*, no.81, March 1966, pp.228–230, reprinted in Archigram, ed., *A Guide to Archigram*, pp.92–93, p.92.

33. Andrew Saint, address to the 20th Century Society's Hayward Gallery symposium, Architectural Association, London 20/3/99.

In 1962 Crompton, Herron and Chalk left the LCC for Taylor Woodrow Construction, on Theo Crosby's invitation. Crosby, a pivotal figure of the London arts scene, was assembling a team for the rebuilding of Euston Station, and later that year he added to the team three more architects: Cook, Webb and Greene. Thus the two 'pools' of Archigram were formally joined into one. The team's massive Euston project, one of the largest of its time, was never to see the light of day, yet the intensity of the creative 'sub-culture' permitted by Crosby at the Euston site hut was undimmed, fuelled by copies of *Architectural Design* and *Architecture d'Aujourd'hui*. Cook was able to draw up his crystalline, geodesic, Bowellist design for a Montreal Tower knowing that Crosby was

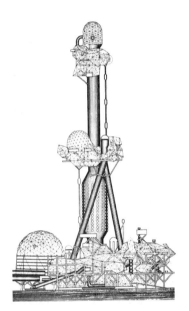
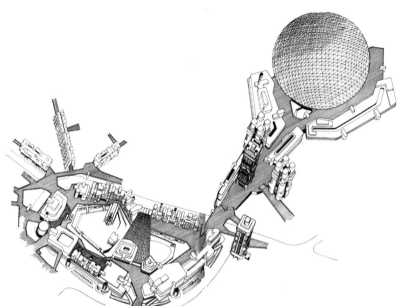

Figure 9. Peter Cook for Taylor Woodrow, Montreal Tower project, elevation, 1963

Figure 10. Taylor Woodrow Group, Axonometric drawing of central area, *Urban Renewal: Fulham Study*, 1963

prepared to take it to the organisers of the 1964 Montreal Expo as a project for a central feature (in the manner of the 1951 Powell and Moya Skylon at the Festival of Britain). Working for the industrial muscle of Taylor Woodrow made even megastructural developments, like the 1963 Fulham Road Study, a heady possibility.

Its monolithic, irregularly-shaped and round-cornered shops, offices and flats were grouped in the mode established by Chalk, Herron and Crompton, but in the way that the development terminated in a gigantic glassy geodesic dome, it showed the influence of Cook, Webb and Greene. Here was evidence that Archigram was thinking as a group, regardless of whose name (in this case, Herron's) appeared on the final drawings. The Fulham project was also the group's last involvement with urbanism in a traditional, massive, and indeed Brutalist sense. Though the Fulham scheme was included in the group's 1963 *Living City* exhibition at the Institute of Contemporary Arts (a decisively avant-garde intervention set up at the suggestion of Crosby), the rest of the show concentrated on the regeneration of modern life through 'non-architectural' means – everyday life, consumption, technology, atmospheres. It was a springboard into a world without mass.

12 | I was Lord Kitchener's Valet or, How the Vic Soc Saved London

GAVIN STAMP

PRIVATE EYE

incorporating THE FLESH'S WEEKLY

VOL I No 4   Wednesday 7th February 1962   Price 6d.

BRITAIN'S
FIRST
MAN
INTO
SPACE

ALBERT GRISTLE
AWAITS
BLAST-OFF

ho ho very satirical

I was Lord Kitchener's Valet or, How the Vic Soc Saved London

GAVIN STAMP

This is a personal and self-indulgent view of a mythic decade. But when Alan Powers first asked me to discuss the 1960s and the growth of the conservation movement, he suggested that I think about it in a much wider context and be autobiographical. 'You were there, after all', he said. And so I was.

I am a child of the Sixties. A child, please note: I was twenty years old in 1968. Later in that momentous year I was, as a second-year history undergraduate, about to use the new Cambridge History Faculty Library designed by the late James Stirling. And I was looking forward to doing so. I saw it, I remember, as a modern equivalent of the mid-Victorian Gothic buildings I so admired, a sort of Butterfieldian protest against good taste and the bland. I now cannot quite remember how I came to think of it in those terms: possibly it was an article by Mark Girouard, but I cannot now trace it. Pevsner said something of the same in his introduction to *The Anti-Rationalists* published in 1973. But my point is that I saw it in these neo-Victorian terms in 1968. Well, how very cruelly was I disappointed: the failings of that arrogant, childish protest formed my subsequent view of architecture – but that is another story.[1]

What I find interesting now is how very absorbed I was by the nineteenth century. At that same moment, the autumn of 1968, I – with Richard Wildman – founded the Cambridge University Victorian Society. The previous vacation I had gone on a grand tour – not to France with my parents as they wanted me to – but to the cities in Britain they had never told me about, let alone showed me. I felt strongly that I should get to know my own country, so I went north to see the great Victorian cities, then so wonderfully, velvety *black* – Birmingham, Manchester, Leeds, Newcastle, Glasgow. For a native Southern Englishman, they were an exhilarating shock.

My interest in the Victorian Age was of some years' standing, developing, I think, from a fascination with the American Civil War. At Dulwich College, I had come to love the 1860s red brick and terracotta buildings by Charles Barry junior and had taken to exploring the surrounding nineteenth-century South London suburbs and to drawing the special railway architecture insisted upon by Alleyn's College of God's Gift. And, in 1966 (no, I have no memory whatever of the World Cup that year: school taught me to detest *all* sport), as a most tiresome callow schoolboy, I joined the Victorian Society – so becoming, I think, the youngest member. The first visit I went on was to St Pancras Station in November 1966. Along with King's Cross, it was then threatened with demolition and Roderick Gradidge – who showed us around – had prepared a scheme for the 'Vic Soc' showing how St Pancras Chambers could easily be converted back into an hotel.

Now, I claim no especial virtue in all this. I was but a child of my time, and what interests me now is *why* I was so interested in the mid-Victorians. What had I been reading? Who influenced me? Well, I know that Betjeman's *First & Last Loves* made a great impression, as did *Nairn's London*, that admirable, personal guide which, I recall, I bought at the Elephant and Castle in 1966.[2] Did

1. see Gavin Stamp, 'The Durability of Reputation: On the Cambridge History Faculty', *Harvard Design Magazine*, Fall 1997, pp.54–7.

2. John Betjeman, *First and Last Loves*, London, John Murray, 1952; Ian Nairn, *Nairn's London*, Harmondsworth, Penguin Books, 1966.

Figure 1. The cover of the fourth issue of *Private Eye*, 7 February 1962, using a photograph of the Albert Memorial by Lucinda Lambton. (Private Eye)

I then notice the modern buildings there by my later friend Ernö Goldfinger? I fear not: they were the sort of new hideous concrete architecture I instinctively hated, and it is a rich – and necessary – irony that I now find myself happily and sincerely defending such buildings.

But it is the question of the climate of opinion which influenced me that I want to pursue. After all, a year or two earlier my interests had been rather different: I had been a precocious marching member of CND, a subscriber to various protest magazines, angry about Regional Seats of Government, and, in my bell-bottom jeans and sleeveless leather tunic, I played my LPs of the droning dirges of Bob Dylan incessantly, to my poor mother's distress. But I had got all that stuff out of the way by 1966: it must be understood that one was nothing if not *avant-garde*.

What, I think, I was part of was the great sea-change in public attitudes, a major cultural shift, which occurred in the first half of the 1960s. And the two parameters are London railway stations. For in 1961–62, the Euston Arch, that supreme and sublime monument of the Railway Age, had been wickedly and unnecessarily demolished – despite the strenuous protests of the Victorian Society. Ultimately the responsibility for what J.M. Richards in the *Architectural Review* called the 'Euston Murder' was the Prime Minister, that cynical, philistine Whig, Harold Macmillan – whom I am perfectly happy to believe was also a war criminal: these things go together. The loss of the Euston Arch was never forgotten, or forgiven, so that by 1967 British Railways found it impossible to eliminate St Pancras (together with King's Cross). A flurry of publicity, combined with the upgrading of the listing of both Barlow's stupendous train shed and Gilbert Scott's Midland Grand Hotel to Grade I, saved both stations. It was a signal victory. By then, of course, Macmillan had long departed as Prime Minister – a victim, in part, of the growth of satire and of cultural changes which are, I believe, intimately connected with the change in attitudes to Victorian architecture and the rise of the Victorian Society.

Serious interest in the Victorians of course goes way back, at least to the 1930s. In 1951 there was a reduced model of the Crystal Palace at the Festival of Britain, as well as Rowland Emett's Railway in Battersea Park which I think reflects the attitudes of the time to the Victorian Age, also manifested in films like that masterpiece *Kind Hearts and Coronets*, and the *Titfield Thunderbolt*. As for Victorian architecture, it had a conspicuous defender in H.S. Goodhart-Rendel, the author of *English Architecture since the Regency* and an architect who gave practical expression to the knowledge of the Victorians he admired in his churches of the 1950s.[3] (This would not happen again until the 1970s with such vaguely neo-Victorian buildings as Hillingdon Civic Centre and Barly Splat at Liskeard, the house built for the artist Graham Ovenden.)

Even so, a serious interest in Victorian buildings was largely confined to an elite. There were Jim Richards and Nikolaus Pevsner at the *Architectural Review*, writing articles which concentrated more on the engineering side – the 'Functional tradition.' Others were more interested in the theatre and other arts of the nineteenth century. This can be explored in the tantalising annual editions of the *Saturday Book*, founded in 1941 and later edited by John Hadfield. Here could be found features by Olive Cook and Edwin Smith on amusing but none the less significant aspects of the Victorian Age. Essentially, all this represented an interest in 'Victoriana', but serious articles appeared on such Victorian cultural manifestations as fairgrounds and popular art. In the world of formica and picture windows, however, these things remained a minority interest.

In response to a small but growing interest in Victorian design, the Victorian Society was founded in 1958. Oddly enough, however, apart from wartime casualties, very few significant examples of Victorian architecture had been destroyed by this date; as Mark Girouard has pointed out, 'it is remark-

THE VICTORIAN SOCIETY

1961   REPORT   1962

Figure 2. The front cover of the *Victorian Society Annual Report* for 1961–2 showing the Euston Arch

3. H.S. Goodhart-Rendel, *English Architecture Since the Regency*, London, Constable, 1953, and see Alan Powers, ed., *H.S. Goodhart-Rendel 1887–1959*, London, Architectural Association, 1987.

able how relatively few good Victorian buildings were demolished. They survived for reasons of economics rather than of taste. Victorian buildings were relatively new, superbly solid, still in mint condition and mostly used for the purposes for which they had been built.'[4] Although there were some serious (and unnecessary) losses in the 1950s, like the Imperial Institute in London (apart from its campanile) and Alfred Waterhouse's Eaton Hall, it was only at the end of the decade that really serious threats to the architectural legacy of the Victorian Age emerged.

Many of the founders of the 'Vic Soc' had been involved with establishing the Georgian Group twenty years earlier.[5] And it is worth noting that a few modern architects were interested, like Hugh Casson and Robert Furneaux-Jordan. At the Society's first Annual General Meeting in 1959, the chairman, Lord Esher, assured members that 'there is plenty to be done, if we had the power and the influence to do it … at present, no one listens to what we say, and "Oh, it's only Victorian" means that it can be ruthlessly destroyed. But it is exciting, I think, to be just in time to save what will be admired tomorrow. The Victorian period, so much laughed at and despised, has ceased to be old-fashioned and has acquired historical charm and distinction. I have lived long enough to see it go through all its stages, from one to the other – admired when it was made, laughed at in the intervening period, and now coming back into favour again. The lovely clothes they wore – even down to so late as *My Fair Lady* – the pictures they painted, their houses and their interior decoration will, I am perfectly convinced, be the rage of the next generation, and it is to us, we happy few, that they will owe there being anything left for them to admire.'[6] And how right he was.

From the beginning, the Victorian Society understood the importance of educating a wider public to achieve its aims, and perhaps its success in this was demonstrated by the comparative youthfulness of its membership. As Nikolaus Pevsner – who had succeeded Esher as Chairman in 1963 – later put it, 'when my generation … tries to explain the *raisons d'être* of certain features in architecture and art, which seem to us to need explanation and even apology, the young lap up just these features with easy and natural relish … [and] have no difficulties over Butterfield or E.B. Lamb. And take recent events at St Pancras. A few years ago only a small band of the initiated would have stood up for it. And there were not enough of them to prevent the unnecessary, the criminal destruction of the Euston Propylaea [sic]. Now not only does our trusted ministerial friend Lord Kennet stand up for it, but Prince Philip's interest in its future implies respect for the building … You will notice that in this I reckon Prince Philip and Lord Kennet among the young, and I hope they will accept that from me. The youth of the sympathisers and of the Society itself has one consequence which I have personally always found particularly attractive. The Vic Soc is an informal society. People who go on our walks and outings and attend our tours and conferences often comment on this. Those who take part talk easily to each other, and friendships are contracted.'[7] You see, the Victorian Society was the world of the 1960s in microcosm; there was Youth and informality. It was not stuffy at all.

The Victorian Society soon enlisted the support of young historians, who were taking the Gothic Revival very seriously. In fact, there was soon a conflict within the society between what one might describe as the *Victoriana Tendency* – essentially finding Victorian architecture 'amusing' and really preferring Classical buildings – and those interested in what historians now portentously called High Victorian Gothic (John Betjeman once asked what was 'Low Victorian'). Although there was a particular social and political edge to this divide (the Goths often being left-wing academics), perhaps this is analogous to the division in our own Twentieth Century Society between the Art Deco trainspotters and those of us who have advanced our interests into

4. Mark Girouard, 'The Evolving Taste for Victorian Architecture', in *Apollo*, February 1973, p.129.

5. see Gavin Stamp, 'The Art of Keeping One Jump Ahead: Conservation Societies in the Twentieth Century,' in Michael Hunter, ed., *Preserving the Past: the Rise of Heritage in Modern Britain*, Stroud 1996.

6. *The Victorian Society: First Annual Report 1959–1960*, pp.4–5. The musical of *My Fair Lady* was first staged in 1956 and the film released in 1964.

7. *The Victorian Society Annual Report 1967–8*, pp.4–5.

the Fifties and even the Sixties.

Nevertheless, the Vic Soc's first major battle was over a Classical structure: the so-called Euston Arch. In 1959 John Summerson had been commissioned by the British Transport Commission to write an architectural history of Euston Station. The resulting booklet was printed but never in fact published as its appearance might have impeded British Railways' plan to rebuild the station.[8] The story is well known. The important point is that the demolition of Hardwick's Greek Doric propylaeum in 1962 was entirely unnecessary. It could have been moved nearer the Euston Road, as the Georgian Group had demonstrated to my great-uncle and the London, Midland & Scottish Railway in 1938 when the station was first threatened with rebuilding; but, as the Vic Soc complained, 'none of the public bodies concerned, neither the Transport Commission nor the London County Council nor the Ministry of Works nor the Treasury, were prepared to foot the bill. This was estimated by the Transport Commission at £190,000 – rather less than the Treasury ungrudgingly paid out about the same time for the purchase of two rather indifferent Renoirs, which no one was threatening to destroy.'[9] As always in our snobbish culture, paintings are valued more highly than architecture even though buildings are more vulnerable as they cannot (easily) be moved.

The campaign to save the Arch culminated in a deputation to the Prime Minister. As Jim Richards later recalled, 'Macmillan listened – or I suppose he listened; he sat without moving with his eyes apparently closed. He asked no questions; in fact he said nothing except that he would consider the matter. A statement was issued later to the effect that the Government had decided not to intervene.'[10] At the same time a mendacious *Times* editorial was published under the title 'Not Worth Saving' written by the editor, Sir William Haley. Such was the sheer malice towards those who fought for the Arch that the demolition contractor, Valori, was prevented from numbering the stones for possible re-erection. All this was never forgotten, or forgiven. And the controversy was important as it saw an alliance – for the last time? – between conservationists and modern architects: Richards' editorial on 'The Euston Murder' in the *Architectural Review* was included in a valedictory book published by Alison and Peter Smithson in 1968.[11] Naturally the familiar argument had been used that the new station would be a worthy replacement, but can anyone really defend the new Euston? Fortunately, it has not been listed – indeed, it would only have got past English Heritage's Post War Steering Group over my dead body.

The next battle came soon after. This was for the Coal Exchange in the City of London, with its extraordinary internal circular cast-iron structure. The excuse for removing it was a road widening, but this was not the real reason. The City Corporation behaved scandalously badly – even worse than usual – and Bunning's building came down in 1962. It was another defeat but, as the Victorian Society's annual report put it, 'We believe that even our lost battles are not altogether fruitless, for on each occasion, successful or not, we recruit more and more disciples to the cause of protecting the best Victorian and Edwardian architecture. Soon we hope thereby to turn the forces of public opinion so much in our favour that no one will dare to allow such needless destruction.'[12]

Ignorant and superficially fashionable prejudice against Victorian design necessitated the society having to deal with many other cases in these years. One was the Hereford Cathedral Screen by Gilbert Scott and Francis Skidmore, one of many good nineteenth century creations cast out in the 1960s. (Fortunately the pieces went to the Victoria & Albert Museum and today this spectacular piece of Victorian metalwork has been restored and is on display.) Many other buildings had to be defended. These included: the Oxford Museum, Bridgewater House, the Waterhouse building at Balliol College,

8. At least one copy survives, now in the possession of the author.

9. *The Victorian Society Report 1961–1962*, p.3.

10. J.M. Richards, *Memoirs of an Unjust Fella*, London 1980, p.127.

11. Alison and Peter Smithson, *The Euston Arch and the Growth of the London Midland and Scottish Railway*, London, Thames and Hudson, 1968.

12. *The Victorian Society Report 1961–1962*, p.1.

Pugin's Scarisbrick Hall, and the National Provincial Bank in Bishopsgate. It surely now seems incredible that any of these could have been seriously threatened with demolition, so when smug modern architects tell us that conservation has gone too far, it is worth remembering this list.

The Society's next major battle was for the Foreign Office. '"I have therefore decided to demolish the existing building." Thus spake Mr. Geoffrey Rippon, present Minister of Public Buildings and Works ... Has Mr. Rippon not noticed that Whitehall and the circumference of St James's Park form the ceremonial scenic centre of one of the great capitals of the world ... The Foreign Office block ... ranks high among these buildings and is, moreover, something that most of us have known and loved all our lives ... We are continually told of the discomfort in which the inhabitants work. Though many of us work in far worse conditions, we have never disputed this. We believe that our suggestions are practical ...'[13] Indeed they were: to keep the facades and Scott's grand reception rooms while creating modern office accommodation on the site. So why was it all going to go? The reason was Sir Leslie Martin's plan for Whitehall, published in 1965; that is, his great scheme for a National and Government Centre – often referred to but seldom illustrated. This is a pity as it can serve as an awful warning and a salutary lesson, for most of the buildings of Whitehall were to be wiped out in favour of an efficient bureaucratic machine. It is worth remembering the breathtaking technocratic arrogance of the conception: what a wonderful symbol of British democracy it would have been if realised.

As I have said, revisionism about the often-derided Sixties is timely and necessary, but it should not go too far. We need to remember that not only was so much of the architectural production sheer rubbish, but that architectural ambition, when allied to the utopian mania for comprehensive redevelopment, could be arrogant to the point of megalomania. Indeed, by the end of the decade, Modern Architecture had become a form of *Terror*, a systematic assault on city after city, which drove many people like me into an uncritical hostility and into conservation. Yes, often the designers were terribly sincere, doing things for the best, seized by a utopian vision; but if there is one thing the 1960s taught me it was to regard such idealism with deep suspicion. I believe in Original Sin. But I digress. The essential point is that the Foreign Office still stands. Bureaucratic inertia survived long enough for the Government to wake up to the fact that it was not a liability but an asset. Now it is very proud of it. In the 1980s the false ceilings were taken down and the whole building has since been both modernised and superbly restored – just as the Vic Soc said could be done, but with even more of Scott's and Digby Wyatt's work retained.

THE VICTORIAN SOCIETY
1965 · ANNUAL REPORT · 1966

Figure 3. The front cover of the *Victorian Society Annual Report* for 1965–6 showing the Hereford Cathedral Screen

Figure 4. A model of the redevelopment proposals by Sir Leslie Martin, from *Whitehall. A Plan for the National and Government Centre*, HMSO, 1965

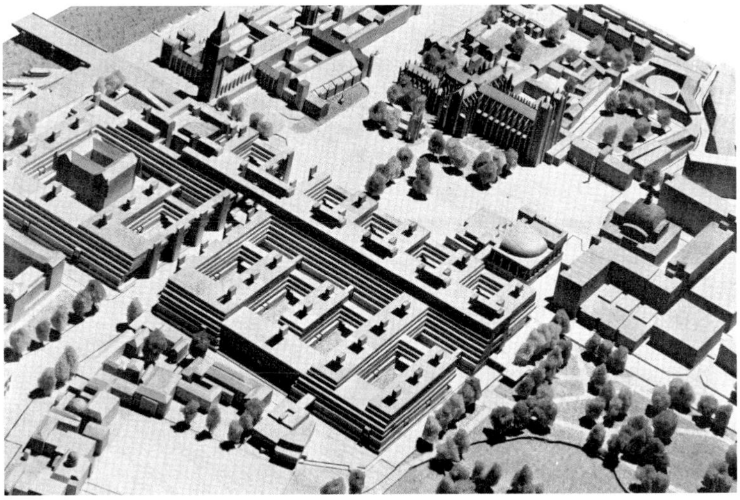

13. *The Victorian Society Report 1963–1964*, p.8.

THE VICTORIAN SOCIETY
ANNUAL REPORT 1966

Figure 5. The front cover of the *Victorian Society Annual Report* for 1966, showing interior of the Midland Grand Hotel at St Pancras Station

14. *The Victorian Society Report 1962–1963*, p.2.

15. John Betjeman, 'Temple to an Age of Steam', in the *Weekend Telegraph* magazine, n.d. (*c.* September-November) 1966, pp.44–48.

16. Betjeman to Summerson, 14 June 1966, in Candida Lycett-Green, ed., *John Betjeman Letters, volume two, 1951 to 1984*, London 1995, p.319; John Summerson in the *Illustrated London News*, ccli, October 1967. See also Nicholas Taylor in the *New Statesman*, 21 October 1966, p.601, and the same writer's devastating attack in the *Sunday Times*, 24 September 1967; headed 'Uninhabitable Cities', it began: "Those who intend to destroy our cities feed us first with lies, damned lies and artists' impressions ..."

17. *The Victorian Society Report 1962–1963*, p.1.

By the time the Victorian Society had to fight its next big battle, attitudes had begun to change. So when the demolition of both St Pancras and King's Cross Stations was proposed in 1966, it didn't happen. 'The change in climate ... cannot be denied, and the Society can claim some credit for helping to bring it about. Taste may have been moving that way inevitably, but the Society has helped to accelerate it, both by its corporate activity, its visits, protests and exhibitions, and by the influence of its individual members. Increasing numbers of people, societies and official bodies are consulting it. The Press is beginning to take it seriously, and little digs about 'Betjemaniacs' and so on now appear comparatively seldom.'[14]

That public opinion had shifted can be seen from the press coverage the controversy generated as well as by the publication of Jack Simmonds's book on *St Pancras Station* in 1968. Two years earlier, John Betjeman had published an article on 'Temples to the Age of Steam' in the *Sunday Telegraph* colour magazine in which he claimed that, 'More damage has been done to London and our other old towns by 'developers' and their tame architects than ever was done by German bombing. No one can object to the clearance of what is shoddy and badly built. St Pancras Station and its hotel, now called Midland Chambers, are neither. It is horrible to contemplate such careful work being destroyed to be replaced by what we are sure to be told is a masterpiece, but will all too probably be like every other new slab along the Euston Road. The Victorian Society is fighting for St Pancras. Let us hope it will be saved ...'[15]

Typically, Betjeman was self-deprecatory about the effect his writings might have. In a letter to 'Coolmore' (i.e., John Summerson), he claimed that, 'It is no good my writing about Sir Gilbert [Scott] and St Pancras in particular, because I have been so denigrated by Karl Marx [J.M. Richards], and the Professor-Doktor [Pevsner] as a lightweight wax fruit merchant, I will not carry the necessary guns.' Summerson at first could not agree, replying, 'No, I just couldn't put any heart into the idea of preserving it,' but later he changed his mind and published 'a cool appraisal' of St Pancras in the *Illustrated London News*. This was characteristically detached and lukewarm, though at least in favour of keeping it.[16]

This battle for St Pancras in 1966–67 is the last Vic Soc case I want to refer to. The Society had won; public opinion really had changed. As it had claimed a few years earlier, 'The Age of Lytton Strachey is over. The Victorians are no longer treated as a joke; they have become fashionable, and even respectable. Exhibitions of Victorian pictures are sure of a good attendance. Publishers hunger for books on Victorian subjects ... Young architects are as likely to be admirers of Butterfield as of Le Corbusier. Young dramatists litter their stage sets with Victorian bric-a-brac. A young film star [Richard Harris] has sprinted off the rugger fields of *This Sporting Life* to buy William Burges's house in Melbury Road ... Antique dealers are hot on the Victorian trail, and in Chelsea, Hampstead and Kensington the throw-outs of the last generation are being honorably reinstated. Only in the more remote and savage parts of the country – in the drawing-rooms of aldermen and property tycoons, in the offices of borough-engineers and cabinet-ministers – has the wind of change scarcely ruffled the (Georgian-style) curtains.'[17]

In trying to chart this wind of change, it is interesting to note what was published at the time. Of particular significance was the first of the 'colour sections', the *Sunday Times* magazine which, edited by Mark Boxer, first appeared in February 1962. From the beginning, this contained serious articles on aspects of the 19th century of a sort – and length – that no Sunday newspaper would dream of considering now: articles of several thousand words, sometimes carried over six or more pages. For instance, there was 'Who were the Victorians? A major series ...' in 1968. Then there were features on Victorian photography, such as the 'Special issue: the Camera', in 1966 (particularly

Special issue: **THE CAMERA**

plus Papa Hemingway, part 2.

Figure 6. The cover of the *Sunday Times* magazine, 18 September 1966

Figure 7. The front cover of *William Morris, Selected Writings and Designs*, edited by Asa Briggs, Penguin paperback, 1962

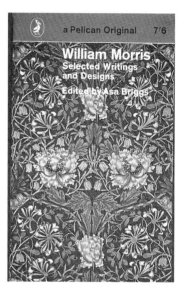

poignant, considering how Helmut Gernsheim's collection of early photographs had recently been offered to and rejected by the British government, so ending up at Austin, Texas, in 1964). As a schoolboy, I cut out and collected all these articles. The *Sunday Times* led in this field, but other newspapers followed suit in their own magazine supplements. *The Observer*, for instance, published 'The Forging of the North' on the Industrial Revolution and northern cities in 1966.[18]

Then there are other cultural markers, like exhibitions on Victorian painters. Ford Madox Brown was celebrated at the Walker Art Gallery in Liverpool in 1965 and Millais at the Royal Academy in 1967. In that same year, two exhibitions were held in London about Victorian church art and plate – scarcely a trendy subject.[19] And all the time there were books being published. Several were on William Morris: Asa Briggs's selection of his writings and designs, issued by Penguin in 1962, and Philip Henderson's and Paul Thompson's studies, both published in 1967. No wonder Morris began to have such an impact on modern wallpaper design. Then there were new and serious histories of Victorian architecture, that is, the collection of essays edited by Peter Ferriday in 1963 and Robert Furneaux Jordan's (rather old-fashioned) Penguin history of 1966.[20] Surely it was significant that the collector and design historian, Charles Handley-Read, began to dispose of his Regency items in the

18. *Sunday Times* magazine, 28 January 1968 and 18 September 1966; *Observer Magazine*, 30 January 1966.

19. 'Copy or Creation – Victorian Treasures from English Churches', organised by Shirley Bury at Goldsmiths' Hall and the Exhibition of Victorian and Edwardian Church Arts organised for the Victorian Society and the Council for the Care of Churches at All Hallows', London Wall, by Anthony Symondson and John Gordon-Christian.

20. Asa Briggs ed., *William Morris, Selected Writings and Designs*, Harmondsworth, Penguin, 1963; Philip Henderson, *William Morris, his life, work and friends*, London, Thames and Hudson, 1967; Paul Thompson, *The Work of William Morris*, London, Heinemann, 1967; Peter Ferriday, ed., *Victorian Architecture*, London, Jonathan Cape, 1963; Robert Furneaux Jordan, *Victorian Architecture*, Harmondsworth, Penguin, 1966.

early Sixties and began to concentrate on the mid nineteenth century, and on William Burges in particular.

Through all these years, the *Saturday Book* carried on, although it would barely survive the decade. No.28, for instance, published in 1968, had an Edwardian lady on the cover contrasted with a dishy model in a Union Jack swimsuit. In addition to an illustrated article by William Gaunt on 'Nineteenth-Century Nudes,' it contained a feature by John Betjeman on the 'Gothic Visions of Rodney Hubbuck' with illustrations of that artist's compelling and precise Pearsonian fantasies. (Earlier editions of the *Saturday Book* had carried the enchanting neo-Victorian drawings of Tom Greeves, soon to become the

NOBLEMAN'S TENEMENT (Coll. John Upfold, Esq.)

The Gothic Visions of Rodney Hubbuck

THE STRANGE and haunting drawings of Rodney Hubbuck are mostly in soft lead pencil. They need no colour. He was for some months a perspective artist in the office of the architects Seely and Paget, but these drawings are something more than ordinary architectural perspectives. They are learned in every detail. I expect, too, that these imaginary buildings would all stand up even without such wooden shoring as is shown in 'Sunken Sanctuary'.

Rodney Hubbuck was born in 1940 at Hindhead and at the age of fourteen went to Frensham Heights, a co-educational school in Surrey. At this merry place his passion for architectural drawing was encouraged and he had annual exhibitions of his work. His native Sussex-Hants borders play a large part in his life. In the drawing on page 234, for instance, look at that Surrey-Hants or Sussex village church sitting calmly in the background of a correct piece of Gilbert Scott most unexpectedly placed and capped with a post-war pyramid and cross. The drawing on page 229 he calls 'Through a needle's eye: an imagined approach to the London, Brighton and South Coast religion'. Indeed, down that narrow alley, with its Ile de France gateway, one does seem to be going past a huge, Anglo-Catholic church on the left, with castle walls on the right, towards a cathedral by R. C. Carpenter, the architect of Lancing College. In the distance is suggested the sunlit English Channel. 'Sunken Sanctuary' has hints about it of Lancing College chapel, should ever that soaring edifice sink into a pocket of the Downs.

Hubbuck delights in strange juxtapositions, and has lately dis-

by John Betjeman

Figure 8. The front cover of the *Saturday Book*, No.28, 1968, designed by Michael Brett

Figure 9. A page from 'The Gothic Visions of Rodney Hubbuck' by John Betjeman in the *Saturday Book*, No.28, 1968

21. For Tom Greeves, founder of the Bedford Park Society in 1963, see his *Ruined Cities of the Imagination*, Malvern, 1994.

22. Nicholas Taylor, 'An 1865 Victorian Rococo Grill Room and a 1905 Art Nouveau City of London Public House', in *The Compleat Imbiber, An Entertainment*, no.8, 1965.

saviour of Norman Shaw's Bedford Park).[21] A similar publication was the *Compleat Imbiber* edited by Cyril Ray, and in 1965 it carried an article by that astonishing and Protean talent of the 1960s, Nicholas Taylor, on the Café Royal and the Black Friar Pub.[22] Taylor, fresh from Cambridge, wrote much on Victorian architecture at this time, in the *Architectural Review* and elsewhere, as well as organising pioneering events for the Vic Soc and ranting at villains like Archbishop Dwyer of Birmingham.

Now I don't say any one of these publications is significant; I merely put them down as markers. And there are others, like the dark, perverse drawings of the American Edward Gorey. These owed much to the drawing style of Victorian illustrators like Tenniel, while Gorey's humour was essentially English. In such recondite little books of the early Sixties as *The Fatal Lozenge, The Hapless Child* and *The Doubtful Guest*, he was laughing and yet not laughing at the Victorians (actually the Edwardians, with their huge fur coats and high stiff collars), and doing so in a new way. Then there was the publication in 1964 of the English edition of Mario Praz's magnificent *Illustrated History of Interior Decoration* – by Thames & Hudson (who else?). Books dealing with nineteenth-century interiors had not been done quite like this before and this volume illustrated rich, cluttered interiors, in colour, and took them seriously. Such images represented the antithesis of modernist austerity.

Indeed, modern architects may have carried on creating austere, bland white interiors, but at a popular level this aesthetic was being rejected – and even by younger architects. Margaret Richardson, whose husband is an architect, tells me how in the 1960s they suddenly started painting walls brown – which was, of course, a Victorian colour. This recollection is confirmed in the novel by Muriel Spark, *The Girls of Slender Means*, published in 1963 but set in 1945 when she imagined 'the drawing room whose mud brown walls appeared so penitential in tone at that time – for the members were not to know that within a few years many of them would be lining the walls of their own homes with paper of a similar colour, it having become smart.'

White walls, for the truly discerning, were out, as was the bare, spare interior preached by the architectural profession. Instead, there was a growing taste for clutter, for richness and darkness and all the qualities once associated with the Victorian Age – with horror. Such effects were enhanced by using objects bought in the Portobello Road to furnish interiors, like old enamelled signs, wax fruit under glass domes and other Victorian relics, together, perhaps, with old posters. The real point is that decoration had become respectable again, and this had a lot to do with collecting – not smart art but Junk. Perhaps all this is summed up by the name of that celebrated shop in Carnaby Street: *I was Lord Kitchener's Valet*.

The new shops in Carnaby Street not only sold trendy gear; they also sold Victorian things. I remember going there as a schoolboy and buying plates from the *Builder* and other nineteenth-century prints for practically nothing. It all went with Dressing Up. Here military uniforms were important: tight-waisted tunics, with frogging, as worn both by stall-holders in the Portobello Road and by pop stars. For, of course, the supreme manifestation of this is that much-illustrated 1967 LP sleeve for the Beatles: *Sergeant Pepper's Lonely Hearts' Club Band* by Peter Blake and Jann Haworth. But why did Victorian uniforms come into vogue? That it was part of a new dandyism is suggested by films like *The Charge of the Light Brigade*, released in 1968: it was full of nice uniforms – with frogging – but it was also important in its attention to accurate period detail, and it was enlivened by animated scenes drawn in the style of Tenniel. The designer was Julia Trevelyan Oman, later the wife of Roy Strong, the director of the National Portrait Gallery, whose contemporary treatment of the Victorian galleries there also comes into this story.

Films are certainly an index of what was happening, for there was also *Oliver!*, also released in 1968. Then there was television, with the BBC's 1967 adaptation of Galsworthy's *Forsyte Saga* referred to enthusiastically in a Victorian Society annual, Ken Russell making his memorable films about such Victorian figures as Elgar (1962) and Rossetti (*Dante's Inferno*, 1967), and Murray Grigor's pioneering study of Charles Rennie Mackintosh (1968). I am sure that John Betjeman's television appearances had a great deal to do with changing attitudes to the 19th century. In this context it is worth remembering what John Summerson had to say about Betjeman in his de-mythologising address to the Vic Soc's AGM in 1968: 'His story … is a mystery of our times and it may be that, as in some other things, we are too close to it to understand. Betjeman has not written even one book about Victorian architecture nor ever to my knowledge promoted any general claims for its qualities. Yet his name has become an illuminant and a sanction; through him, kindliness towards Victorian architecture is permitted to thousands whose habits of mind would drive them in a quite other direction.'[23] There was *First and Last Loves*, of course, but, even so, it is still difficult to chart that extraordinary man's influence.

With decoration being taken seriously again, interest grew in a building type which is half architecture and half interior design. I refer to pubs which – unlike housing estates or university buildings – must respond directly to

Figure 10. Four pages from *The Fatal Lozenge* by Edward Gorey, New York, 1960

23. John Summerson, 'The Evaluation of Victorian Architecture', in *The Victorian Society Annual 1968–9*, pp.45–6, reprinted in Summerson, *Victorian Architecture: Four Studies in Evaluation*, New York and London, 1970.

popular taste – as Roderick Gradidge never tired of pointing out. What was happening in Sixties pub design was a deliberate rejection of modernity, for what a successful pub needs is a sense of enclosure, darkness, colour, glitter, richness: all things *verboten* in earlier decades. Curiously, this practical revival of interest in Victorian gin palaces began in the 1940s in the *Architectural Review*, whose editors created the Bride of Denmark 'pub' in the basement in Queen Anne's Gate, filled with acid-etched mirrors, old pub fittings, Staffordshire pottery and a stuffed (half) lion.[24] Pub interiors designed by Gradidge in the 1960s like The Bull at Highgate exploited this neo-Victorian tendency, while the Three Greyhounds in Soho of 1968 was decorated like a church interior by Ninian Comper, with stencilled painted decoration using strong colours (now

Figure 11. Interior of the Three Greyhounds in Soho by Roderick Gradidge and decorated by Campbell, Smith and Co., completed in 1969 (the late Roderick Gradidge)

Figure 12. Interior of the Clarendon Arms in Islington, designed (and photographed) by Roderick Gradidge (the late Roderick Gradidge)

all destroyed or painted out, alas). Then there were the remodellings in *c.*1962 of the Hornsey Wood Tavern and the Clarendon in Islington by Gradidge which were affected by the new taste for Art Nouveau.

Now, the Art Nouveau Revival was very important indeed, and was intimately connected with the revival of interest in decoration and in 19th century design. In 1965 the *Sunday Times* magazine carried an article on 'Taste '95 … The Art that Launched a Thousand shops.' 'Two or three years ago,' it claimed, 'a few shillings could buy an example of Art Nouveau, the decorative style which flourished between 1890 and 1910 – even on shop and stall fronts. Today it is the height of fashion. Is this just another vogue? …' In the same

24. See Roderick Gradidge, 'False Pretences', in *Time Gentlemen Please!*, SAVE Britain's Heritage, 1983; and Ben Davis, *The Traditional English Pub*, London 1981. The Bride of Denmark has now gone, but the Victoria, Strathearn Place, Paddington, survives as a pioneering example of this modernist approved neo-Victorian.

issue, the artist Bernard Cohen maintained that Art Nouveau 'was the first flowering of the avant-garde attitude, and at the same time a commercial and popular success.'[25] And so it was again in the 1960s, having a palpable influence on new revivalist wallpaper designs. Naturally, there were those who were profoundly disturbed by this decadent tendency. Anguished editorials appeared in the Design Council journal. For what worried the upholders of the purity of whiteness and modernity was that intellectuals, artists and designers had become seriously interested in decoration again. Something was happening.

As far as I can see, Art Nouveau made decoration and pattern intellectually respectable again. The two significant markers were exhibitions at the Victo-

ria & Albert Museum. The first was in 1963, devoted to the illustrations of the Bohemian poster designer, Alphonse Mucha; the second, in 1966, rehabilitated the decadent draughtsmanship of Aubrey Beardsley. Both were the work of Brian Reade, who published his major study of Beardsley's work the following year. The *Sunday Times* had a great splash on Beardsley in the colour magazine.[26] And here posters are important: both the reproductions of images by Mucha, Beardsley, Toulouse-Lautrec and others published by companies like Athena and the new 'psychedelic' posters which – together with record sleeve designs – were strongly influenced by Art Nouveau. As Bevis Hillier noted in 1969, 'Art Nouveau and Beardsley meant "decadence" and it was therefore natural that the "beautiful people" and the "flower children" of the pop-music, drug-taking, drop-out culture should adopt Art Nouveau as its graphic style.'[27]

Perhaps the most public expression of the Art Nouveau Revival was a shop – a most fashionable one: Biba, in its many manifestations. In these, Barbara Hulanicki brought several tendencies together to present an alternative rich

Figure 13. A double-page spread from 'Taste '95' in the Sunday Times magazine, 21 November 1965

25. *Sunday Times* magazine, 21 November 1965.

26. *Sunday Times* magazine, 8 May 1966.

27. Bevis Hillier, *Posters*, London 1969, p.273; also see Maurice Rickards, *The Rise and Fall of the Poster*, Newton Abbot, 1971, p.38 etc.

141

naughty world to the young – sybaritic, luscious, luxurious. The decadence of 1890 was fused with the style of 1920s; there was colour, sensuality, richness. Furthermore, this commercial enterprise linked up the designer world of the Art Nouveau revival with popular youth culture and psychedelic experiences: it all came together in Biba. And surely it is simply impossible to smoke dope in a white room – let alone try LSD. Blowing your mind requires colour, decoration and profusion. Modernity was unthinkable; indeed, the ideal of the Modern Movement was alien to the contemporary drug culture. This was demonstrated by the dark interiors used in *Performance*, the notorious film starring Mick Jagger which was finally released in 1970 but shot in that fateful year 1968.

My essential point is that the story of the Sixties is not simple. The culture of the decade was not uniform, but reflected several different but interlocked worlds. As far as architecture is concerned, the decade saw the beginning of a wholesale rejection of the manifestation of the sterile uniformity and internationalism of the Modern Movement. Suddenly it was old-fashioned. You can see this in, say, the writings of Ian Nairn and the worries beginning to be expressed about destruction of cities through comprehensive redevelopment.[28] There was a widespread feeling against landlords and property developers – not just the odious exploiter Rachman but also shady characters like Rudolph Palumbo who were making lots of money by putting up mediocre,

28. The evolving, angry opinions of Ian Nairn (1930–83), the best architectural writer and broadcaster of the decade, are of great significance here; his article, 'Stop the Architects Now' in the Weekend Review of the *Observer*, 13 February 1966, provoked a paranoid hurt response from the RIBA: see my article on Nairn in the forthcoming *New Dictionary of National Biography*.

Figure 14. The front cover of *Art Nouveau and Alphonse Mucha* by Brian Reade, Victorian & Albert Museum exhibition catalogue, London, HMSO, 1963

crass buildings. And then there was the scandal of Harry Hyams erecting Siefert's Centre Point – and leaving it empty. All this came to head in late 1960s – and it is surely significant that Oliver Marriott's book on *The Property Boom* was published in 1967.[29]

What is particularly interesting is that a reaction against 1960s high-rise public housing began very early. Although it was not built until later, Darbourne & Darke's competition-winning design for the comparatively low-rise and artfully picturesque housing in Lillington Gardens in Westminster dates from as early as 1961 – that is, almost before the 1960s industrial system-building juggernaut had got going. The design in red brick seemed to take its cue from the colour of G.E. Street's Italian Gothic church of St James the Less standing proudly in the middle of the development. Pevsner was impressed by this: 'So here is the architectural style of 1960 proclaiming its appreciation of the style of 1860. This is, I need hardly say, very gratifying to us committed Victorians. Nor should we really be surprised to see this sympathy. After all, the Gropius-Mies-SOM style went with clean-shaven faces, but both 1860 and 1970 are bearded generations. But this is by the way.' And also outside my period, as this quote dates from 1973.[30]

For I want to end this crude attempt at cultural history in that polemical year 1968, as things had so greatly changed since 1961. 1968 was also the year of the Mackintosh Exhibition (shown both in London and Edinburgh) which can be seen as both an end and a beginning: a beginning as it represents a wider popular appreciation of a sometimes neglected figure; an end because Toshie was no longer presented merely as a Pioneer of Modern Movement but also as a Victorian exponent of art nouveau decoration. Robert Macleod's important book on the architect of the same year took this argument further by demonstrating that Mackintosh was what he was because he had roots in past as well as being of his time.

Another great British architect celebrated his centenary the following year, in 1969. This was Edwin Lutyens, but he received rather less attention than Mackintosh mainly because attempts to mount an exhibition at the RIBA were rubbished by Peter and Alison Smithson, denigrating his non-modernist achievement from the Olympian Heights of their own self-promotion. So Lut had to wait until 1981 to receive his due, but others – mainly in the Victorian Society – were beginning to take him seriously.[31] Nicholas Taylor and Roderick Gradidge organised pioneering tours of his houses in 1967 and 1968. I remember going on them, and feeling the sheer excitement of being really *avant-garde*, at the cutting edge of architectural history.

So what else was happening in 1968? There was the explosion at Ronan Point, of course, which now seems a turning point in both the design of public housing and in conservation. By end of decade, nobody who was truly progressive still believed in Modern Architecture. 1968 is certainly a key year as things were coming together: there was a convergence of interests between the world of the Victorian Society and a wider popular culture. We all dressed up in uniform then, after all – John Lennon and I, we had that in common. And 1968 was also the moment when I like to think the Sixties and I parted company. I had no particular interest in student protest, and despised the shallowness of my colleagues who went to Grosvenor Square with ball-bearings to put under the hooves of the police horses. I never felt I belonged to the Sixties, and it was only in the 1970s that I learned how to behave badly, as well of course as descending into Young Fogeydom, and worse … But the story is not quite that simple; it never is, not least as I now find myself defending buildings I automatically and unthinkingly loathed (or, rather, did not understand or really *see*) over thirty years ago. This is right and proper: we must all move on, and learn new tricks. I am part of the Sixties nevertheless, in all the attitudes I had, and have, I think. We cannot escape our own time, our moment. And these days, *pace* my

29. Oliver Marriott, *The Property Boom*, London, Hamish Hamilton, 1967; Centre Point was completed in 1966.

30. Nikolaus Pevsner, 'Elective Affinities', in *The Victorian Society Annual 1972–73*, p.4.

31. see Gavin Stamp, 'the Rise and Fall and Rise of Edwin Lutyens', in the *Architectural Review*, vol.170, November 1981.

old tutor and mentor David Watkin, I believe in the dear old *zeitgeist*. So I am part of the 1960s: not the Sixties of myth, not the Sixties as selectively remembered by fading modern architects, but a more complex, rich and interesting historical period.

It was the decade that saw the beginning of the rejection of the Modern Architecture which had become so established in the 1950s, in the Macmillan years. It was the decade when the Vic Soc was at the cutting edge of research, with young historians and enthusiasts investigating Street and Butterfield, William White and Henry Woodyer, S.S. Teulon and Edward Buckton Lamb, let alone Charles Rennie Mackintosh and Edwin Lutyens. It was also the decade of Art Nouveau, and all of these things were pushing forwards the boundaries of acceptable taste. And it was the decade which saw an amazing and profound change in public opinion towards the attitudes and artefacts of the Victorian period – just as the Society had hoped for and predicted at the beginning.

Well, today the dear old Vic Soc carries on, perhaps a little like an ageing pop-star – still doing the same thing, but with rather less relevance and purpose. Perhaps that is true of most of us. So many of the battles have long been won. Even so, bliss was it in that dawn to be alive, back in the 1960s – the Decade of the Vic Soc.

I should like to record my debt to the late Roderick Gradidge and to the late Edwina Porter as well as to Rosemary Hill, Nicholas Oddy and Andrew Sanders for their help in preparing this lecture.

Figure 15. Cambridge University Victorian Society Dinner, 1971:
Back row: Francis A.C.S. Bown, Andrew Sanders, Michael Pick;
Front row: Anthony Symondson, the author, David Watkin